Malnutrition

Titles in the Diseases and Disorders series include:

DISEASES & DISORDERS

Malnutrition

Don Nardo

LUCENT BOOKS

An imprint of Thomson Gale, a part of The Thomson Corporation

THOMSON

GALE

Detroit • New York • San Francisco • New Haven, Conn. • Waterville, Maine • London

LIBRARY OF CONGRESS CATALOGING-IN-PUBLICATION DATA

Nardo, Don, 1947-
  Malnutrition / by Don Nardo.
      p. cm. — (Diseases and disorders)
  Includes bibliographical references and index.
  ISBN-13: 978-1-59018-677-0 (hardcover)
  1. Malnutrition—Juvenile literature. I. Title.
  RC623.N37 2007
  616.3'9–dc22   2007006795

ISBN-10: 1-59018-677-X
Published in the United States of America

Table of Contents

"The Most Difficult Puzzles Ever Devised"

Charles Best, one of the pioneers in the search for a cure for diabetes, once explained what it is about medical research that intrigued him so. "It's not just the gratification of knowing one is helping people," he confided, "although that probably is a more heroic and selfless motivation. Those feelings may enter in, but truly, what I find best is the feeling of going toe to toe with nature, of trying to solve the most difficult puzzles ever devised. The answers are there somewhere, those keys that will solve the puzzle and make the patient well. But how will those keys be found?"

Since the dawn of civilization, nothing has so puzzled people—and often frightened them, as well—as the onset of illness in a body or mind that had seemed healthy before. A seizure, the inability of a heart to pump, the sudden deterioration of muscle tone in a small child—being unable to reverse such conditions or even to understand why they occur was unspeakably frustrating to healers. Even before there were names for such conditions, even before they were understood at all, each was a reminder of how complex the human body was, and how vulnerable.

While our grappling with understanding diseases has been frustrating at times, it has also provided some of humankind's most heroic accomplishments. Alexander Fleming's accidental discovery in 1928 of a mold that could be turned into penicillin has resulted in the saving of untold millions of lives. The isolation of the enzyme insulin has reversed what was once a death sentence for anyone with diabetes. There have been great strides in combating conditions for which there is not yet a cure, too. Medicines can help AIDS patients live longer, diagnostic tools such as mammography and ultrasounds can help doctors find tumors while they are treatable, and laser surgery techniques have made the most intricate, minute operations routine.

This "toe-to-toe" competition with diseases and disorders is even more remarkable when seen in a historical continuum. An astonishing amount of progress has been made in a very short time. Just two hundred years ago, the existence of germs as a cause of some diseases was unknown. In fact, it was less than 150 years ago that a British surgeon named Joseph Lister had difficulty persuading his fellow doctors that washing their hands before delivering a baby might increase the chances of a healthy delivery (especially if they had just attended to a diseased patient)!

Each book in Lucent's Diseases and Disorders series explores a disease or disorder and the knowledge that has been accumulated (or discarded) by doctors through the years. Each book also examines the tools used for pinpointing a diagnosis, as well as the various means that are used to treat or cure a disease. Finally, new ideas are presented—techniques or medicines that may be on the horizon.

Frustration and disappointment are still part of medicine, for not every disease or condition can be cured or prevented. But the limitations of knowledge are being pushed outward constantly; the "most difficult puzzles ever devised" are finding challengers every day.

A Global Problem with Many Faces

The term *malnutrition* refers to a serious medical condition caused by an insufficient or improper diet. Essentially, a person who suffers from malnutrition takes in too few nutrients—vital vitamins, minerals, and/or proteins—to sustain the body's normal functions and a state of good health. If the condition goes untreated, serious illness and even death can result.

When people who live in developed, industrialized nations hear the word *malnutrition*, they often visualize starving people in undeveloped, third world countries. In one sense, this is appropriate. Some 850 million people, living mainly in the world's poorest nations, do not get enough to eat each day. They make up more than one-seventh of the world's total population. Hundreds of millions of them suffer from nutritional deficiency diseases such as scurvy and beriberi. Moreover, each and every day more than sixteen thousand children die of hunger-related causes, translating into the loss of one child every five seconds. In sheer numbers, therefore, malnutrition is by far the most widespread deadly medical condition in the world.

Groups Adversely Affected by Malnutrition

Despite these staggering and tragic figures, however, they do not reflect or capture the true scope of the overall threat that malnutrition poses to human populations and societies. Indeed, the specter of world hunger is only one aspect of a problem that is more far-reaching and insidious than most people realize. First, a simple lack of food—sometimes called undernutrition—is not the only cause of malnutrition. Eating too much food of little nutritional value—sometimes referred to as overnutrition—can also make the body malnourished and lead to health problems. Most people in developed nations like the United States have enough to eat; however, poor nutrition is widespread and growing in many of these countries. So they are not immune to the debilitating effects of malnutrition, which experts say is a global, rather than localized, problem. According to the World Health Organization (WHO), malnutrition

Approximately 850 million people, living mainly in the world's poorest nations, do not get enough to eat each day.

A group of women and children wait for food to be distributed at a camp in Sudan. There are ongoing efforts all over the world to end mass starvation.

covers a broad spectrum of ills, including undernutrition, specific nutrient deficiencies, and overnutrition; and it kills, maims, retards, cripples, blinds, and impairs human development on a truly massive scale worldwide. Despite significant improvements in world food supplies, health conditions, and availability of educational and social services, because of the fundamental role nutrition plays in attaining and preserving health, no population escapes malnutrition's grasp. All countries have significant population groups with some form of debilitating malnutrition.[1]

The amount of food a person eats and the nutritional quality of that food are not the only factors contributing to malnutrition in rich and poor countries alike. Disease, especially cancer, can cause malnutrition, for example. Also, people who abuse alcohol and other drugs or who suffer from depression and other emotional problems are highly susceptible to becoming malnourished. Thus, cancer patients, heavy drinkers, and individuals with clinical depression are among the local population groups that WHO says suffer disproportionately from the effects of malnutrition. Children also have a greater-than-average chance of being malnourished. Even those from affluent families with full refrigerators tend to be uneducated about proper nutrition and too often fill up on sweets and other nonnutritious foods.

People with eating disorders also have a high risk of experiencing malnutrition and its debilitating effects, including weight loss, fatigue, damage to the immune system, organ dysfunction or failure, and, in the severest cases, death. Eating disorders occur everywhere. But they are particularly prevalent in affluent nations, including the United States. For a variety of reasons, some of those afflicted with these disorders purposely reduce their food intake, in effect starving themselves. Doctors estimate that 15 to 20 percent of these individuals end up dying of malnutrition, despite the fact that they have ready access to plenty of nutritious food.

Still another population group adversely affected by malnutrition is the elderly. People in their sixties or older are more likely than younger people to experience various social, psychological, and physical conditions and problems that can result in malnutrition. Among these problems, of course, is poverty, which exists to some degree in every nation; the fact is that some elderly people just do not get enough to eat. However, malnutrition in aged populations has many other causes. In the words of one medical expert, these include the

> inability to shop, cook, or feed oneself. Two percent of persons aged 65–84 years require assistance with feeding. This figure rises to 7 percent for persons aged 85 years or older. In the 75 to 84 years age group . . . 16 percent need help with food preparation and 29 percent need assistance

with shopping. In nursing homes, failure to pay attention to ethnic food preferences may result in food refusal and [malnutrition]. . . . Dementia [brain dysfunction] is also commonly associated with [malnutrition]. Older persons with dementia often forget or refuse to eat. . . . [In addition] diseases that interfere with the ability of the person to eat or to prepare food, such as stroke, tremors, or arthritis, can all lead to decreased food intake.[2]

These and similar problems are so common, in fact, that a recent study found that as many as a third of the elderly patients in U.S. nursing homes may be malnourished.[3]

A Preventable Condition

Thus, malnutrition has many faces. It can and does affect people in every country, in all economic groups, and in all age groups. Virtually everyone is at risk of suffering from the condition, depending on one's changing physical, social, and/or economic circumstances.

Fortunately, the symptoms of malnutrition are known and easily recognizable. Furthermore, medical tests and treatments of various kinds are available in nearly all hospitals; in a majority of cases, the harmful effects of the condition are reversible. In more affluent countries, local efforts to fight malnutrition consist first of identifying the high-risk groups— heavy drinkers, the elderly, people with eating disorders, and so on. When and where possible, medical and governmental authorities educate members of these groups about the dangers of malnutrition and offer them treatment.

Meanwhile, on the larger scale of world hunger, the United Nations (UN) and other international organizations are engaged in an ongoing effort to end mass starvation. Those involved in this effort recognize that it is huge, difficult, and will likely take many years to complete. Yet the experts agree that there is hope because the goal is ultimately reachable. "The ravages caused by malnutrition on individuals, families and societies are preventable," a recent UN report emphasizes, and "the measures needed to reduce and end it are increasingly understood."[4]

CHAPTER ONE

The Kinds and Causes of Malnutrition

The World Health Organization defines malnutrition as "the cellular imbalance between the supply of nutrients and energy and the body's demand for them to ensure growth, maintenance, and specific functions."[5] In other words, a person with malnutrition is unable to get the nutrients and energy his or her body requires to function in a normal, healthy manner. This serious medical condition has been a major cause of illness and death throughout human history. And even today, in a world with advanced medical knowledge and technology, malnutrition continues to kill thousands of people each day.

Modern medical authorities recognize that two general forms of malnutrition affect these populations. The first, primary malnutrition, occurs when an otherwise healthy person does not consume a sufficient amount of food or specific nutrients to maintain good health. On the one hand, someone might consume too little food overall and as a result lack both protein and essential vitamins and minerals. This form of primary malnutrition is called marasmus. On the other hand, if a person's problem is primarily a lack of protein, he or she can suffer from a form of primary malnutrition called kwashiorkor. Marasmus is the most prevalent form of malnutrition in the world, affecting perhaps close to a billion people, mostly in developing and poorer countries. Kwashiorkor occurs in poorer

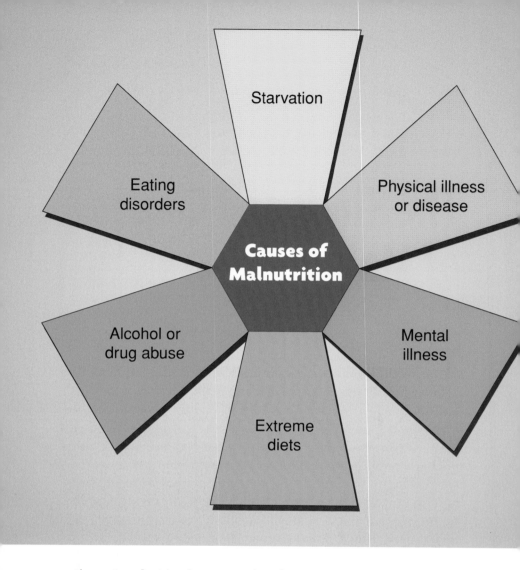

Starvation

Eating
disorders

Physical illness
or disease

**Causes of
Malnutrition**

Alcohol or
drug abuse

Mental
illness

Extreme
diets

nations, too, but is also a growing threat to health in developed
countries, including the United States.

The second general category of malnutrition, secondary
malnutrition, is a common side effect of illness due to disease
or injury. For example, diseases of the kidney, liver, thyroid,
and pancreas can keep the body from absorbing sufficient
quantities of nutrients. This can fairly quickly lead to malnutrition. Similarly, injuries to the bones or major organs or extensive burns to the skin can cause loss of appetite, which can
trigger the onset of malnutrition. Other examples of secondary
malnutrition include extended bouts of fever, major surgical
procedures, and excess diarrhea. Secondary malnutrition can

and does regularly occur across the world, in both poor and affluent nations and societies. Doctors everywhere recognize the dangers of malnutrition and watch for it in their ill patients, both inside and outside of hospital settings.

The Harmful Effects of Malnutrition

The main reason why malnutrition is so dangerous is because it can adversely affect the entire body. The human body requires certain minimal levels of food and nutrients to produce energy and function properly. Failure to maintain these levels results in physical and mental damage, which increases in severity for as long as a person remains malnourished. As

Babies and young children who are malnourished suffer effects such as impaired growth and increased risk of infection.

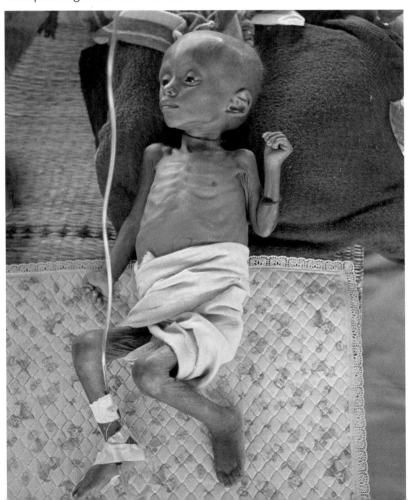

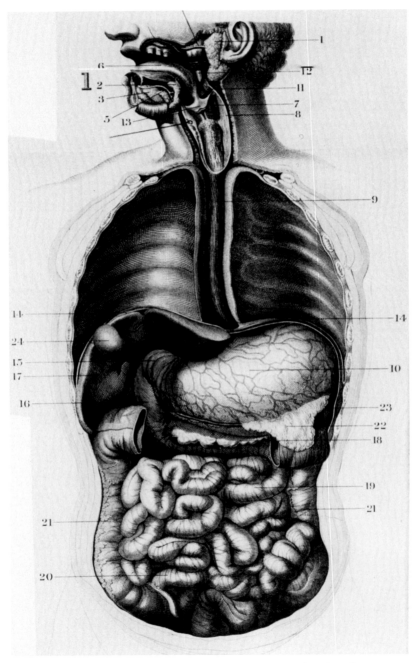

The human body requires certain minimal levels of food and nutrients to produce energy and function properly. Pictured here is the digestive tract of the human body.

Donna G. Grigsby of the University of Kentucky's College of Medicine explains:

> Malnutrition affects virtually every organ system. Dietary protein is needed to provide amino acids for synthesis [creation] of body proteins and other compounds that have a variety of functional roles. Energy is essential for all biochemical and physiologic [mechanical] functions in

The Elderly Are at High Risk for Malnutrition

One of the world's leading group medical practices, the Mayo Clinic (with branches in Florida, Minnesota, and Arizona), says the following about malnutrition and the elderly:

Older single adults, even energetic and self-sufficient ones like your aunt, often don't cook for themselves; unless invited out, their typical dinner may be nothing more than a handful of popcorn or a cup of tea. Carried on for long, a nutrient-poor diet accelerates the loss of muscle mass and strength that normally comes with aging. Shopping and preparing food become more difficult, which reinforces the tendency to subsist on easy but empty fare—toast, cold cereal, saltines. Eventually, the chronic lack of nourishment leads to increased frailty and dependence, which in turn can trigger depression—itself a major drain on appetite. Malnutrition weakens the immune system, increasing the risk of pneumonia and other serious infections and exacerbating existing health conditions. And it can also contribute to mental confusion. Very ill or disorientated people are unlikely to eat well, if at all, and they're more likely to end up in a hospital or long-term care facility, where they're vulnerable to pressure sores, infections, post-surgical complications and further malnutrition.

Staff of the Mayo Clinic, "Malnutrition and Seniors: When a Relative Doesn't Eat Enough." www.mayoclinic.com/health/senior-health/HA00066.

the body. Furthermore, micronutrients [vitamins and minerals] are essential in many . . . functions in the body.[6]

Malnutrition, especially when it occurs over the course of weeks, months, or longer, produces harmful effects on victims of all ages, including fetuses. Sadly, if the mother is malnourished, her unborn child will be too. Lacking sufficient nutrients, a fetus can suffer brain damage or retarded growth and/or be born underweight or even stillborn. If the infant survives and continues to be malnourished, it might experience further retarded growth as well as mental retardation. Other common effects of malnutrition in children include an increased risk of infection (because of an impaired immune system); partial or complete blindness; and anemia, a deficiency of red blood cells, making it harder for the blood to carry oxygen to the body's tissues and organs.

Some of the same ill effects of malnutrition, including anemia and blindness, are observed in adults. Both children and adults can also suffer from acute weight loss, fatigue, and delayed wound healing. Heart disease and diabetes (the body's inability to regulate sugar levels in the blood) are common effects of malnutrition in adults. Also among adults, pregnant women who are malnourished do not gain enough weight, adversely affecting the development of their unborn children. And elderly people who suffer from malnutrition are particularly prone to falling and breaking their hips and other bones. Finally, regardless of their age, all people with malnutrition will experience massive organ failures and death if the condition continues long enough.

Poverty and Alcohol Abuse

In order to avoid these life-threatening effects of malnutrition, experts say, people need to be aware of what causes this body-wasting condition. At first glance, identifying the culprit may seem easy. Across the globe, extreme poverty often leads to the inability of individuals or entire local populations to acquire sufficient food to sustain good health. Indeed, history is replete with examples of mass starvation brought about by poverty. This situation still exists in some of the world's poorer nations.

However, malnutrition also exists—on a smaller but still significant scale—in affluent societies. Even the United States, the richest nation on earth, is not immune to the problem. Some of the malnutrition in America can be attributed to poverty, as pointed out in September 2006 by the *Philadelphia Inquirer*:

> The Food Bank for New York City recently reported that nearly 20 percent of children in the city rely on free food

How Alcohol Affects Digestion

This clear explanation of how alcohol impairs the digestive process, thereby promoting malnutrition, comes from the National Institute on Alcohol Abuse and Alcoholism.

Alcohol inhibits the breakdown of nutrients into usable molecules by decreasing secretion of digestive enzymes from the pancreas. Alcohol impairs nutrient absorption by damaging the cells lining the stomach and intestines and disabling transport of some nutrients into the blood. In addition, nutritional deficiencies themselves may lead to further absorption problems. For example, folate deficiency alters the cells lining the small intestine, which in turn impairs absorption of water and nutrients, including glucose, sodium, and additional folate. Even if nutrients are digested and absorbed, alcohol can prevent them from being fully utilized by altering their transport, storage, and excretion. Decreased liver stores of vitamins such as vitamin A, and increased excretion of nutrients such as fat, indicate impaired utilization of nutrients by alcoholics.

National Institute on Alcohol Abuse and Alcoholism, "Alcohol and Nutrition." http://pubs.niaaa.nih.gov/publications/aa22.htm.

to survive. According to statistics from Bread for the World, 13 million children went to bed hungry in the United States in 2004, the most recent year for which statistics are available.[7]

Though stark and disturbing, these figures do not reflect the actual extent of malnutrition in the United States. Indeed, many people are surprised to learn that poverty is by no means the only cause of malnutrition in affluent countries. Another common cause is alcohol abuse, a widespread problem in such nations. Numerous studies have shown that casual and moderate drinkers show no signs and have little or no risk of becoming malnourished. However, the risk increases significantly for heavy drinkers—those who have several drinks per day, every day.

One major reason why high alcohol consumption can lead to malnutrition is because alcohol is filling and makes most heavy drinkers eat less. High levels of alcohol in the body also damage several of the organs that normally break down and distribute essential nutrients. According to the National Institute on Alcohol Abuse and Alcoholism:

> Alcohol is very rich in energy, packing 7 calories per gram. But like pure sugar or fat, the calories are void of nutrients. The more calories an individual consumes in alcohol, the less likely it is that they will eat enough food to obtain adequate nutrients. To make matters worse, chronic alcohol abuse not only displaces calories from needed nutrients, but also interferes with the body's metabolism of nutrients, leading to damage of the liver, digestive system, and nearly every bodily organ.[8]

Cancer and Liver Disease

Just as excessive alcohol consumption can damage the body and thereby trigger malnutrition, damage caused by certain diseases can have similar results. Among the most destructive diseases in this regard is cancer. Medical experts point out that many different kinds of cancer exist and that some are more likely to cause malnutrition than others. Particularly troubling are gastrointestinal cancers, such as cancer of the esophagus, stomach, and intestines, each of which interferes with normal digestion. Studies show that roughly 15 to 40 percent of patients with these types of cancer suffer from malnutrition during the course of their illness. Even worse are head and neck cancers, which interfere with the eating process itself. More than 40 percent of patients with these cancers become malnourished, sometimes temporarily, other times for long periods.

Besides interfering mechanically with digestion and eating, various cancers can have adverse effects on the body's normal

Stomach cancer can interfere with normal digestion, leading many patients with this type of cancer to suffer from malnutrition during the course of their illness.

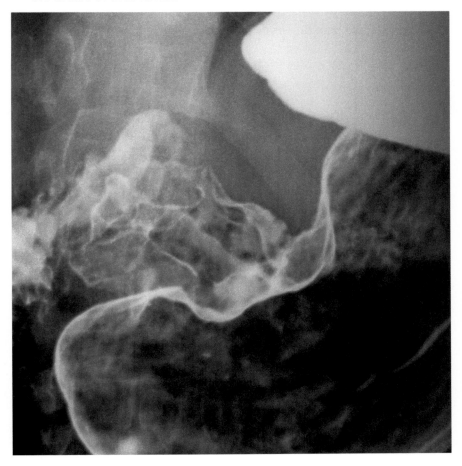

chemical processes. And these effects can lead to a state of malnutrition. Joel B. Mason, an expert on cancer and malnutrition, explains:

> Cancer can cause great changes in how the body metabolizes protein, carbohydrates, and fat. This in itself can be a major cause of weight loss. These metabolic changes work together in ways we still don't quite understand to cause very large reductions in lean body mass, mostly muscle, with much smaller decreases in fat. This is similar to what we see in acutely ill, hospitalized patients and is probably caused by many of the same factors. Because more than 95% of the body's metabolic activity occurs within the lean body mass, loss of lean body mass can have a drastic impact both on the effectiveness of medical treatments and on general health.[9]

Three human liver specimens (left to right): normal, fatty, and cirrhotic.

Liver disease is another frequent cause of malnutrition. The liver is one of the most versatile and vital organs in the body. It produces bile, a secretion that aids in digestion, breaks down toxic substances in the blood, stores some essential nutrients, and processes various proteins essential to building bodily tissues. When the liver is not working correctly, it negatively impacts health. Malnutrition is among the adverse side effects of some forms of liver disease. People with cirrhosis of the liver are especially prone to becoming malnourished. Cirrhosis occurs when scar tissue replaces normal cells in the liver. According to the American Liver Foundation, "People with cirrhosis often experience loss of appetite, nausea, vomiting, and weight loss, giving them an emaciated appearance."[10] To reverse this onset of malnutrition, physicians administer large amounts of protein since cirrhosis interferes with normal processing of protein.

Depression

The effects on the body of eating too little food, consuming excess alcohol, and contracting cancer and other diseases are mainly physical in nature. However, not all of the causes of malnutrition are physical. Some mental illnesses or emotional disturbances can also cause someone to become malnourished.

Among the more serious of these illnesses is depression. According to the National Institute of Mental Health (NIMH), depression (sometimes referred to as a depressive disorder) is

> an illness that involves the body, mood, and thoughts. It affects the way a person eats and sleeps, the way one feels about oneself, and the way one thinks about things. A depressive disorder is not the same as a passing blue mood. It is not a sign of personal weakness or a condition that can be willed or wished away. People with a depressive illness cannot merely "pull themselves together" and get better.[11]

Depression can be triggered by several different factors, among them the death of a loved one, family or money problems, loneliness, assault or rape, and physical illness or hormonal imbalances. Typical symptoms include persistent sadness, feelings of hopelessness, apathy about life, fatigue, difficulty concentrating, thoughts about death, and loss of appetite.

Loss of appetite caused by depression sometimes leads to moderate or severe cases of malnutrition. The adverse effects of malnutrition then make the depressed individual feel even more depressed, so he or she may eat even less and become still more malnourished. Eventually, the person may need to be hospitalized. The number of people who suffer from malnutrition brought on by depression is unknown. But the NIMH estimates that in the United States alone up to 10 percent of the population, or close to 30 million people, suffer from depression at one time or another.

Other Causes of Malnutrition

Medical experts have pinpointed a number of other causes of malnutrition in both poor and affluent societies. More common than most people realize are problems associated with chewing and swallowing. For example, gum disease, advanced tooth decay, and poorly fitting dentures all can contribute to difficulties in chewing. Gum disease and tooth decay can also make food taste bad, discouraging eating in some people. Likewise, a chronic dry mouth, along with other side effects of some diseases and medications, can make swallowing difficult. If one or more of these oral problems persist, malnutrition can result.

Similarly, certain medicines can cause stomach upset or change the way food tastes, discouraging eating and thereby causing malnutrition. The world-famous Mayo Clinic points out that many drugs

> can contribute to malnutrition by suppressing appetite, altering the way food tastes, causing nausea and vomiting, or interfering with absorption [of nutrients by the body]. Offending drugs include some antidepressants, certain blood pressure and anti-osteoporosis medications, and even common analgesics such as aspirin. The problem is often compounded in [elderly people] because many older people take several medications, all of which may affect the ability to eat and digest nourishing foods.[12]

The same sorts of adverse effects are often associated with recreational drug use in which people consume certain nonprescribed or illegal drugs on a regular basis. In many people, for example, repeated cocaine use can suppress appetite and over time make them malnourished. The same is true for certain stimulants, including speed, Ritalin, and ephedra, and for some hallucinogens, such as LSD and ecstasy. An even stronger suppression of appetite occurs when people mix drugs, a practice often called polysubstance use or abuse. A person might abuse cocaine while drinking alcohol and taking in excessive amounts of caffeine (from coffee or soft drinks), for instance. Medical experts say that people who mix drugs this way on a regular basis have a much higher risk of becoming malnourished.

Extreme Dieting

Fad diets or extreme diets are still another cause of malnutrition. The riskiest such diets are those that severely limit what a person can eat and therefore do not promote complete or balanced nutrition. For example, some diets discourage people from consuming foods from one or more of the general food groups (dairy products, meats, vegetables, fruits, grains, and so on). In particular, diets that advocate eating little or no protein can lead to the onset of malnutrition in some people. It is much healthier and more prudent, nutritionists say, to eat moderate amounts of foods from all the major food groups; this approach ensures that a person gets a proper balance of protein, carbohydrates, fats, vitamins, minerals, salt, and other substances essential to good health.

Fad dieting, in which someone who has access to a varied diet purposely restricts his or her food intake, is for the most part an artifact of affluent cultures. Many of these diets, as well as alcohol and drug abuse, produce the same harmful effects as those resulting from extreme poverty and starvation in many third world countries. This demonstrates that malnutrition is a complex, persistent problem with many causes, some of them surprising and subtle. And people everywhere—rich or poor, young or old—can be at risk for acquiring this common and harmful medical condition.

CHAPTER TWO

Recognizing the Symptoms of Malnutrition

Like many other medical conditions or disorders, malnutrition has certain recognizable symptoms, or physical and behavioral signs, that reveal its presence. Yet that does not mean that diagnosing malnutrition is always a straightforward, easy process. First, any given person suffering from the condition may display only some of the classic symptoms. It is actually unusual for someone to display all of them.

Moreover, each of the symptoms of malnutrition is also a sign of several other diseases and conditions. Fatigue, for example, can signal the onset of malnutrition; yet fatigue is also a symptom of low blood pressure, insomnia, liver damage, low blood sugar, and infection, among other problems. Similarly, another common symptom of malnutrition, slow wound healing, is also a sign of poor circulation, diabetes, and infection. Thus, a doctor who suspects that a patient is suffering from malnutrition must conduct a thorough examination and consider the broad spectrum of symptoms.

Another significant factor affecting initial suspicions and diagnosis of malnutrition is the fact that whatever symptoms a patient does display usually do not appear all at once. This is particularly true in developed nations, where the condition is most frequently caused by factors other than out-and-out starvation. According to one prominent public medical resource:

> General malnutrition often develops slowly, over months or years. As the body's store of nutrients is depleted, changes begin to happen at the cellular level, affecting biochemical processes and decreasing the body's ability to fight infections. Over time, a variety of symptoms may begin to emerge.[13]

Malnutrition and Disease

As the noted humanitarian group Doctors Without Borders points out here, malnutrition and disease often go hand in hand because malnourished people are more likely than well-nourished people to contract various diseases.

Children under five years of age are the most at risk because they are growing rapidly and have a hard time fighting off disease. Outbreaks of acute malnutrition have also been linked to measles epidemics. In fact, chronic food insecurity and common diseases often conspire together to exacerbate the situation. Acute malnutrition makes children more susceptible to infection, especially measles. On the other hand, measles can prompt an already malnourished child to stop eating and drinking, throwing the child into a state of acute malnutrition. Pregnant and nursing mothers are also highly vulnerable because they need more calories and nutrients than other adults. Because they are usually isolated and have a harder time accessing food, the elderly are also highly at risk. Like children, adults suffering from acute malnutrition are more susceptible to serious diseases such as respiratory tract infections like pneumonia or whooping cough due to their weakened condition.

Doctors Without Borders, "Acute Malnutrition." www.doctorswithoutborders.org/news/malnutrition/index.cfm.

Weight Loss and Related Symptoms

One of the more common of these symptoms is weight loss. To keep functioning normally, the body needs to burn calories, so it turns to burning calories stored in the tissues. And these tissues steadily disappear as they are burned, causing weight loss. Medical experts generally view a weight loss of 2 percent or more a week, or 5 percent or more a month, as a sign of malnutrition.

Of course, a person who goes on a calorie-reducing diet can exhibit some of the same symptoms of malnutrition. The difference is that whereas the dieter purposely eats less food than normal on a temporary basis, a person suffering from malnutrition loses weight on an involuntary basis. Both malnutrition and calorie-reducing diets can be harmful to the body, in part because of the way the body reacts to having inadequate supplies of food. A common misconception is that when the normal calorie intake is reduced, the body starts burning fatty tissues only. The reality, however, is that in many cases it burns

A young Sudanese girl, lying with her mother, is close to death from starvation.

existing muscle tissue as well. "This is because of famine mechanisms built into our makeup," researcher Alisha Durtschi points out. Essentially, these instincts

> tell the body to use up a good percentage of the muscles first as energy before it uses fat, holding [some of the] fat in reserve for really tough times. . . . Of course, the obvious muscular signs of malnutrition are the lack of muscle tone and in progressed cases, the skeletal look of the body.[14]

In addition to reduced muscle mass, malnutrition can cause retarded growth in infants and children. During infancy and childhood, the body uses a certain amount of food to create new bone, muscle, and other kinds of tissues, thereby causing the person to grow. But when the person is chronically malnourished, he or she lacks the proteins, vitamins, and minerals necessary to stimulate normal growth. And the result is retarded growth, or stunting. "Once you're stunted, the potential for catch-up growth is limited," says Beatrice L. Rogers of the Friedman School of Nutrition Science and Policy. Moreover, stunting is "bad for a host of reasons, such as [loss of] strength [and] stamina, [and] chronic disease risk. It also causes challenges to cognitive [mental] performance."[15]

Anemia and Fatigue

Another frequent symptom of malnutrition is anemia, which is a measurable reduction in the number of red blood cells. Normal levels of red blood cells are vital because these cells carry hemoglobin, an iron-rich protein that brings oxygen to the body's tissues. Anemia can be caused by several other factors and conditions besides malnutrition. So doctors in all nations regularly encounter patients who are anemic to one degree or another. However, malnutrition is by far the most common cause of anemia, particularly in poor and developing countries. According to the World Resources Institute in Washington, D.C.:

> In developing countries, 40 percent of non-pregnant women and 50 percent of pregnant women are anemic, and 3.6 billion people suffer from iron deficiencies. The problem is

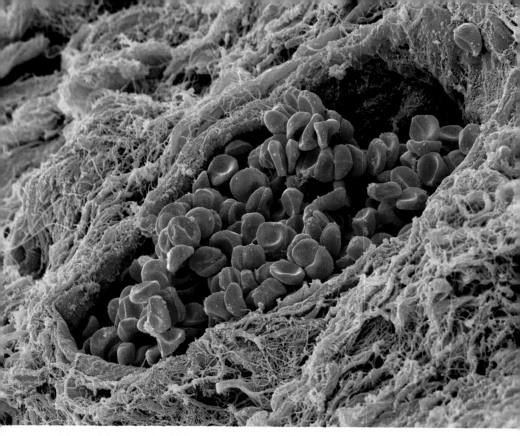

Normal levels of red blood cells, pictured here, are vital because they carry hemoglobin, an iron-rich protein that brings oxygen to the body's tissues.

most severe in India, where 88 percent of pregnant women are anemic. Anemia increases the risk of death from hemorrhage [severe bleeding] in childbirth. Iron deficiencies can also reduce physical productivity and affect a child's capacity to learn.[16]

Both malnutrition and anemia share the symptom of fatigue. When red blood cell and iron levels drop, the heart and some other organs work harder in an attempt to adjust to the loss; similarly, when normal food intake is curtailed, the body begins working overtime to create needed energy in whatever ways it can. These processes, along with other factors, produce feelings of tiredness that tend to become more pronounced over time.

Malnutrition can also cause mental fatigue. Among the organs that become increasingly starved of nutrients in a malnourished person is the brain, the normal functions of which can be adversely affected. Thus, people suffering from malnutrition on a prolonged basis often display symptoms such as dizziness, disorientation, a lack of coordination, persistent confusion, and/or irritability.

Symptoms Related to Protein Deficiency

Just as reduced levels of iron and other nutrients can cause anemia and fatigue, insufficient supplies of protein can have adverse effects on the body and produce telltale symptoms of malnutrition. Frequently, for example, chronic shortages of protein in the diet are revealed by noticeable increases in the amount of time it takes for wounds to heal. "Protein is needed for tissue regeneration and repair," say researchers Douglas MacKay and Alan L. Miller. "A protein deficiency can delay wound healing by exacerbating [prolonging] the inflammatory phase of the wound."[17] (Shortages of vitamins A and C and the mineral zinc, which are also typical in malnourished people, can make wounds heal more slowly as well.)

A lack of protein and other nutrients can also affect the liver in adverse ways. In particular, kwashiorkor, the type of malnutrition characterized by insufficient dietary protein, produces a symptom and condition known as fatty liver (technically known as steatorrhoeic hepatosis). A person suffering from fatty liver experiences an excess buildup of fats in the liver, causing the liver to swell in size and to function abnormally. Most cases of fatty liver due to malnutrition are seen in young children in developing countries. In affluent nations like the United States, by contrast, diagnosing malnutrition can be complicated by the fact that two diseases fairly common in those nations—diabetes and alcoholism—also cause fatty liver.

Another easily recognizable sign of kwashiorkor is a greatly bloated belly, a symptom seen most often in undernourished children in some of the poorer parts of Africa. The humanitarian organization Doctors Without Borders reports that this symptom

often affects children when they are no longer fed milk and their new diet is lacking in protein. The protein deficiency

A recognizable sign of kwashiorkor is a greatly bloated belly, a symptom seen most often in undernourished children.

causes fluids to drain from the blood into the stomach, causing the characteristic swelling (edema) which may also be present in the arms, legs, hands, feet, and faces.[18]

Abnormalities of the Skin

The abnormal fluid accumulation that causes swelling of the stomach, feet, and hands of many chronically malnourished individuals can also manifest itself in the skin. That is, a serious lack of protein can cause fluids to build up in the skin. This can make some parts of the body look somewhat puffy, which can mask the subtle but increasing loss of muscle tissue beneath. Also, as the skin swells, it can feel stretched and tight, and the victim might experience periodic bouts of muscle twitches.

The skin of a malnourished person can also be adversely affected by xerosis, the clinical name for dry skin. If the state of malnutrition persists, the skin can become increasingly wrinkled, cracked, or blotchy, taking on an alligator-skin look. It can also become discolored, appearing various shades of dull yellow or brown.

Still another symptom of malnutrition that can show up in the skin is follicular hyperkeratosis, a condition of the hair follicles. Durtschi describes it this way:

> You've surely seen goose bumps when your skin has been cold. This is a natural reaction by the skin to make the hairs stand up, slowing down the transfer of heat from your skin to the air. There is a symptom very similar to this caused by malnutrition . . . follicular hyperkeratosis.

A malnourished person can be adversely affected by dry skin, whereby the skin can become increasingly wrinkled, cracked, or blotchy.

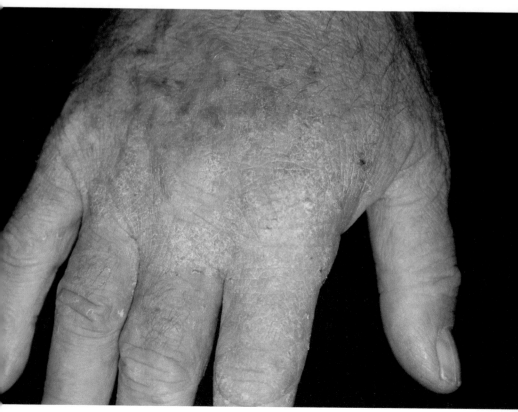

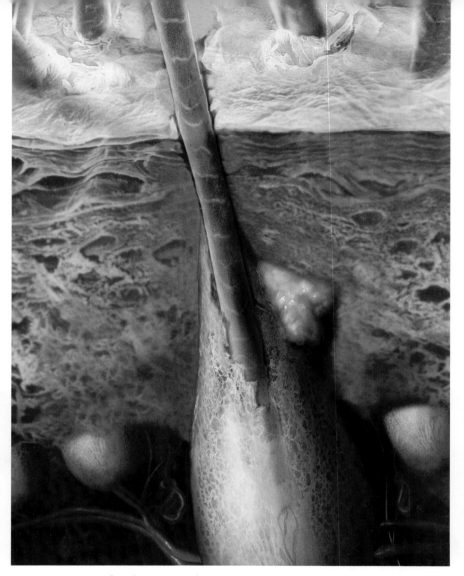

A symptom of malnutrition that can show up in the skin is follicular hyperkeratosis, a condition of the hair follicles.

Only [it] doesn't go away when the skin is warmed. Sometimes it's hard to see this and it's much easier to feel these small bumps by rubbing your hand across the skin. These hard spots are formed in each hair follicle and give the skin a rough feel. The surrounding skin is dry.[19]

Severe Diarrhea and Constipation

Children in poorer, developing countries also frequently display another common symptom of malnutrition—diarrhea. Diarrhea is a physical condition in which a person experiences frequent watery, loose bowel movements. The World Health Organization estimates that as many as 3.5 million people die from uncontrolled diarrhea each year, approximately 80 percent of them children under the age of five. Most cases of severe, chronic diarrhea are caused by infection and disease. However, a significant proportion of these cases are the result of various degrees of malnutrition.

Not only can malnutrition cause episodes of diarrhea, but cases of diarrhea initially caused by infection also can be made worse by poor nutrition. In addition, in a sort of vicious cycle, diarrhea can make malnutrition worse by suppressing appetite. For example, a person can begin to suffer from malnutrition and in time develop the symptom/complication of diarrhea; the diarrhea can then cause a decrease in appetite, which makes the victim eat even less, leading to more serious malnutrition and perhaps more severe diarrhea.

Trouble in the Colon

Diarrhea, often severe, is one of the most common symptoms of malnutrition, especially among children in poorer, underdeveloped countries. The renowned Mayo Clinic provides this clearly worded explanation of the basic processes of diarrhea.

Normally, the food you eat remains in liquid form during most of the digestive process. When the unabsorbed food residue passes through your colon [part of the intestines, in which nutrients are absorbed into the body], most of the fluids are absorbed and what remains is a semisolid stool. In diarrhea, the food and fluids you ingest pass too quickly or in too large an amount—or both—through your colon. The fluids aren't sufficiently absorbed, and the result is a watery bowel movement. In addition, the lining of your colon may be inflamed or diseased, making it less able to absorb fluids.

Staff of the Mayo Clinic, "Diarrhea: Causes." www.mayoclinic.com/health/diarrhea/DS00292/DSECTION=3.

In an apparent paradox (the coexistence of two factors that seem to contradict each other), malnutrition can cause constipation as well as diarrhea. Constipation is a condition in which a person has infrequent and dry, usually hard, bowel movements. When someone is malnourished, he or she can suffer from dehydration, which is a lack of sufficient fluids, as well as eat too little dietary fiber (which aids in digestion and excretion of wastes). Both dehydration and a lack of dietary fiber can trigger constipation. As in any disease or condition, symptoms can vary from one person or group to another. Thus, whereas some malnourished people suffer from diarrhea but not constipation, others experience constipation but not diarrhea. Still others undergo alternating episodes of both, a particularly uncomfortable and physically dangerous situation.

Symptoms of the Head and Face

In addition to adversely affecting the digestive tract, blood, muscles, and skin, malnutrition causes several abnormalities and clearly recognizable symptoms in and around the head. The hair, for instance, can become stiff, wiry, and difficult to manage. The hair can also lose some of its normal pigmentation, sometimes giving the impression that the victim is prematurely graying. (In many black people, the hair turns reddish rather than gray.) Such abnormal changes in hair color are sometimes referred to as a flag sign because they flag, or call attention to, a serious underlying problem, in this case malnutrition. If the onset of malnutrition is relatively quick, the faded, unhealthy-looking hair will be visible near the scalp, while the ends of the hairs will still look normal.

Abnormalities often appear in and around the eyes as well. In some victims, the eyelids become inflamed and swollen. Also, it is common for small, circular grayish spots to appear on the white surfaces near the corners of the eyes. These spots can look dry, dull, or foamy. Durtschi summarizes some of the other symptoms associated with the eyes:

> The inner surfaces of the eye lids can get thicker as well as the outer layer of the eye ball itself. The blueness of the whites of the eyes may disappear. They may also pick up

a wrinkled appearance with the addition of an increase of those small capillary blood vessels that make the eyes look "red." As the symptoms worsen, the thickened outer layers of the eye and inner layers of the eye lid may create a glazed, porcelain-like appearance that can actually hide the small capillaries that are making the eyes red. Holding the eye open and asking the subject to roll their eyes around, you may see what appears like a dull, lusterless, or roughened surface on the eyes, created by that thickened layer of outer tissue.[20]

The mouth can also display telltale signs of malnutrition. On the outside, sores can appear on the lips, and the skin directly above the upper lip can become yellowish and scaly. Meanwhile, inside the mouth the taste buds on the tongue sometimes disappear, and white patches can appear on the tongue. The latter symptom (which is also seen in many advanced AIDS patients) is a sign that the immune system is in distress. Sores can also appear on the gums and inside the cheeks. In addition, it is not unusual for victims of malnutrition to experience more than normal amounts of tooth decay. The teeth can display brown stains and take on a generally corroded look. Finally, because the bones in which the teeth are embedded become fragile, one or more teeth may loosen and even fall out.

Thus, malnutrition can reveal itself through a wide range of symptoms. Because the condition affects every bodily system and eventually nearly every organ, these symptoms can present themselves almost anywhere in the body, from swollen feet below to discolored hair above. Recognizing the classic signs of malnutrition is the first step in diagnosing this debilitating condition. The next and most crucial step in many cases is to conduct certain tests to confirm the suspected diagnosis.

CHAPTER THREE

Testing for and Treating Malnutrition

Although the many and varied symptoms of malnutrition are well known to physicians, not all malnourished people display all of the classic signs. On the one hand, it is common for different victims to display different combinations of symptoms. On the other, even when some of these symptoms appear in a patient, they may not be associated with malnutrition. Thus, the diagnosis of malnutrition is complicated by the fact that most of the symptoms are also signs of other diseases and conditions.

Particularly in developed, affluent countries where mass starvation does not exist, doctors may not be able to definitively diagnose malnutrition from the symptoms alone. They must instead perform various tests to confirm the diagnosis suggested by the symptoms. A number of reliable tests for malnutrition have been developed over the years, ranging from preliminary questionnaires and physical exams to a battery of laboratory procedures.

Once a doctor has firmly determined that a patient is indeed suffering from malnutrition, the next step is treatment. This can vary widely from patient to patient, depending on the severity of the case, the patient's situation and lifestyle, and the medical and nutritional resources available to the patient and physician. In some situations, treatment might be as simple as making sure that the patient has enough food to restore normal levels of health. In others cases, more involved treatments may be necessary, including medicine regimens, nutritional education, and/or psychological counseling.

This full range of treatments for malnutrition is available mainly in developed countries, where medical research and facilities, trained doctors and nurses, labs for running tests, and financial resources to aid in patient recovery are abundant. Perhaps ironically, in such affluent societies a majority of cases of malnutrition go unreported. This is because most people who are malnourished in such societies do not realize it. (In contrast, in poorer countries, where large-scale hunger is common, people know they are malnourished and why.)

Taking a Medical History

Thus, physicians in developed countries are not always immediately aware that some of their ailing patients are suffering from malnutrition. Almost without exception, the first test such a physician does to confirm his or her suspicion of malnutrition is to take a medical history. In fact, as Ramzi R. Hajjar of the Department of Internal Medicine at the University of South Florida puts it, "A carefully obtained history is the most valuable tool for identifying persons at risk for malnutrition."[21] A medical history consists of a series of questions and answers. The doctor asks the patient how long he or she has been ill, whether any added symptoms have manifested themselves, and what medicines or drugs have been recently consumed, along with various questions about the patient's lifestyle. In this way, the physician can pinpoint potential risk factors that might have contributed to the illness and hopefully rule out certain diseases and disorders.

When the doctor suspects that the patient is malnourished, it is particularly important that the medical history include information on recent diet, eating habits, and any medical conditions experienced. For example, Hajjar recommends that the patient provide a "food diary" that lists both the quantity and quality of the foods eaten in recent months. "The history should also ascertain the presence of risk factors for deficient nutrition intake," Hajjar continues, such as poverty, social isolation, and inability to shop, prepare food, or feed. Additionally, any chronic medical condition that may potentially affect nutritional status must be documented, such as diabetes, [heart] disease, gastrointestinal conditions, depression, dementia, and [bone] disease. Acute illnesses may demand increased nutritional requirements, and the frequency and severity of such events must be noted. Review of both prescription and over-the-counter medications is essential to avoid polypharmacy [unwanted and often unsafe duplication of medicines].[22]

This wide-ranging information gives the doctor a much better chance of either confirming or discounting the initial diagnosis of malnutrition.

Administering a Physical Exam

The next step in determining an exact diagnosis is to administer a physical exam. Most physicians will do this as a matter of course, even if they are already 90 percent sure that they know what is ailing the patient. Though not completely definitive by itself, a physical exam might confirm the doctor's initial suspicions, or it might reveal some crucial factor that was not addressed in the medical history.

First, the doctor will check the patient's vital signs, including temperature, blood pressure, and pulse rate, to determine his or her present physical status. Then the doctor will look for traditional symptoms of malnutrition, such as changes in hair color, spots on the eyeballs, sores inside the mouth, swelling of the limbs, and so forth. Another common physical test for malnutrition is to measure the circumference of the arms and calves. These measurements might reveal the loss of muscle mass often associated with the condition. Still another physical test is to measure the thickness of the skin in various areas of the body in order to determine if the patient has normal stores of fat.

The doctor will also weigh the patient. This step can reveal more than simply the amount of weight the person has lost in

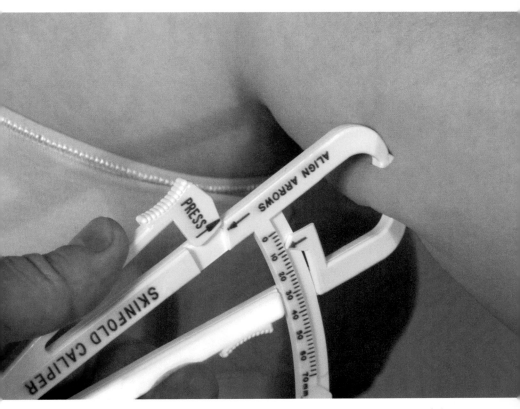

One physical test for malnutrition is to measure the thickness of the skin in various areas of the body in order to determine if the patient has normal stores of fat.

the past few weeks or months. Many doctors use the patient's present weight to calculate his or her body mass index (BMI), which can be an important clue to nutritional status. To obtain someone's BMI, one divides his or her weight (in kilograms) by his or her height (in meters). The resulting figure is therefore an indicator of the relationship between weight and height. And the lower the figure, the more likely the person is to be underweight and undernourished. For people in their twenties, thirties, and forties, a normal or desired BMI ranges from 20 to 24, and a result below 18 suggests a high probability that the person is malnourished. In elderly people, a normal BMI ranges from 24 to 29, with a probability of malnutrition in results below 22 to 24.

Lab Work: Blood Tests

If the diagnosis is still uncertain after the completion of a physical exam, the physician will order one or more laboratory tests that can confirm a malnourished state. Among these lab tests are some standard kinds of blood work. And for diagnosing malnutrition, the most commonly administered blood test is called a serum albumin test. Albumin, a substance manufactured in the liver, keeps the blood from leaking out of the body's blood vessels and also contributes to tissue growth and healing. A serum albumin test reveals the levels of albumin in the blood. If the levels are below normal, it might show that the liver is malfunctioning, which itself is a symptom of malnutrition; in addi-

The Serum Albumin Test

A leading online source of medical information provides these facts about the serum albumin test, frequently used to diagnose malnutrition.

This test helps in determining if a patient has liver disease or kidney disease, or if not enough protein is being absorbed by the body. Albumin is the protein of the highest concentration in [blood] plasma. Albumin transports many small molecules in the blood (for example, bilirubin, calcium, progesterone, and drugs). It is also of prime importance in maintaining the oncotic pressure of the blood (that is, keeping the fluid from leaking out into the tissues). This is because, unlike small molecules such as sodium and chloride, the concentration of albumin in the blood is much greater than it is in the extracellular fluid. Because albumin is synthesized by the liver, decreased serum albumin may result from liver disease. It can also result from kidney disease, which allows albumin to escape into the urine. Decreased albumin may also be explained by malnutrition or a low protein diet.

A.D.A.M., "Serum Albumin Test." http://findarticles.com/p/articles/mi_adm4445/is_8/ai _n16083009.

tion, low albumin levels can indicate low levels of protein in the body, which is another common sign of malnutrition.

Another common blood test that aids in diagnosing malnutrition is the serum cholesterol test. Cholesterol is a fatty substance that moves through the blood by attaching itself to protein. Normal amounts of cholesterol in the blood aid in constructing new cells and in manufacturing various hormones. Higher-than-normal levels of cholesterol in the blood increase the risk of heart attack because excess cholesterol can clog the arteries. In contrast, lower-than-normal levels of cholesterol can signal inadequate supplies of protein, which is a strong indicator of malnutrition.

In addition to tests that measure levels of albumin and cholesterol in the blood, several other blood tests are available to test for malnutrition. For instance, a complete blood count measures, among other things, the volume of red blood cells in the body. Low levels of red blood cells can indicate anemia, a common result of malnutrition.

Other Lab Tests

Some doctors who suspect that a patient might be malnourished will order other lab tests, either in addition to or instead of blood tests. Among these are urine tests. In a urine test, the patient submits a sample of urine and the lab uses portions of the sample for one or more tests, one of which measures the amount of urea present. Urea is a waste product that forms when proteins break down. If protein levels are abnormally low, as is the case with most malnourished people, urea levels will be correspondingly low, so that low urea levels can be an indicator of malnutrition.

Another urine analysis tests for ketones in the urine. Ketones are substances that form when the body burns its own stores of fat to produce energy. In healthy, well-nourished people, the body has plenty of protein and other nutrients to burn. But a malnourished body has to resort to burning the fat stores (along with some muscle tissue), which releases ketones. Thus, unusually large amounts of ketones in the blood are a classic sign of malnutrition.

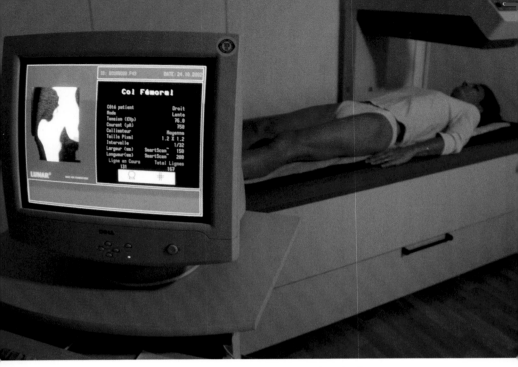

A patient's bone density is examined by using the dual energy X-ray absorptiometry machine.

Still another lab test that can reveal the existence of malnutrition is the X-ray, specifically when it is used to examine bone density. A healthy person who consumes adequate quantities and types of nutrients usually has a certain acceptable bone density. However, a malnourished individual often consumes inadequate amounts of calcium, magnesium, copper, and zinc; deficiencies of these substances can reduce bone density, making bone tissues thinner and more susceptible to damage. The present X-ray procedure of choice for examining bone density is dual energy X-ray absorptiometry, which can detect a change in bone density as small as 1 percent.

Treatments: Food Supplements and Medicines

Once the doctor has concluded his or her tests and is sure that the patient is suffering from malnutrition, the next step is to institute some sort of treatment. For some malnourished patients, particularly those with mild or moderate cases of malnutrition, treatment may be as simple as increasing food intake.

To increase food intake properly and safely, a physician prescribes dietary supplements. These typically include increased amounts of protein, balanced with appropriate quantities of vitamins and iron and other minerals. In developed countries like the United States, patients with mild or moderate cases of malnutrition are most often given detailed instructions on what foods to buy and eat. They then follow these instructions in the privacy of their own homes. At the same time, the doctor will require them to attend several follow-up appointments in the ensuing months, to ensure that the new dietary plan is proceeding as it should.

However, in cases of severe malnutrition, the patient is most often hospitalized, at least for an initial period. That way, trained medical personnel can monitor the patient's food intake and overall health several times a day. A clinical setting also makes it possible for doctors and nurses to be able to respond quickly to any sudden physical complications, such as liver or

A computer read-out of a bone density test.

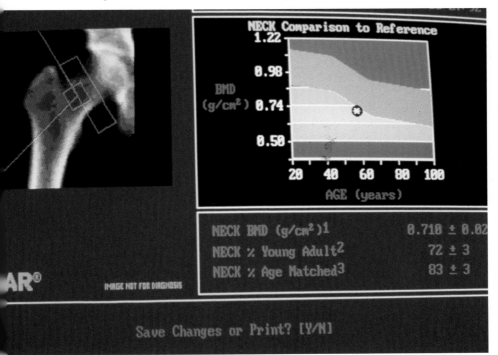

heart failure, which may occur in the early stages of recovery. In such situations tube feeding is sometimes required, especially among severely malnourished children, elderly persons, and patients suffering from anorexia (self-induced starvation).

Sometimes, for example in the cases of elderly persons who become malnourished while living in rest homes, giving a patient adequate food and urging him or her to eat it are not completely effective by themselves. The patient may, for a variety of physical and/or psychological reasons, have lost his or her appetite. And that may be a primary reason for the patient's malnourished condition. In such situations, doctors can administer medicines that stimulate the appetite. Megestrol acetate, a kind of steroid, has proven to be effective in increasing appetite among malnourished patients suffering from cancer and AIDS. And another steroid, nandrolone, has been used to increase appetite in and improve the nutritional status of patients whose kidneys are failing.

In addition, as reported by Hajjar, an expert on malnutrition among the elderly, "Growth hormone has been shown to stimulate weight gain in severely malnourished older patients." However, he cautions, "Growth hormone is extremely expensive." Another drawback is that treatment of malnutrition with growth hormone "for more than six months has been associated with a variety of [unpleasant] side effects."[23] In fact, the consensus of medical experts is that such medicines should not be used as a first line of defense against malnutrition; rather, they should be administered only in situations in which other forms of treatment are ineffective.

Individual Therapy and Support Groups

It should be emphasized that treatments for malnutrition involving increased food intake and appetite stimulants and other medicines will work only if the patient is willing to go along with said treatments. Some malnourished people resist normal treatments because of psychological reasons. They may, for instance, have some kind of eating disorder that makes them feel fat even when they are extremely thin; so they may refuse to eat even when the doctor says they should. Another example is people who have, for one reason or another, lost the will to live. There are also people who have a great deal of trouble following drastically new eating, cooking, shopping, and other behavioral regimens and need help in reorganizing their lives and learning new, more healthy habits.

People in these situations sometimes benefit from psychological counseling (or psychotherapy), which consists of individual therapy, group therapy, or both. In individual therapy, a counselor, who is a caregiver specially trained to deal with people with food and eating issues, meets with the patient on a regular basis for several months. The counselor helps the patient to better understand why and how he or she became malnourished in the first place and how much better his or her life will be after successful treatment. Over time, hopefully, the patient learns to overcome, or at least to cope with, his or her food issues.

A nutritionist counsels a patient about healthy eating habits.

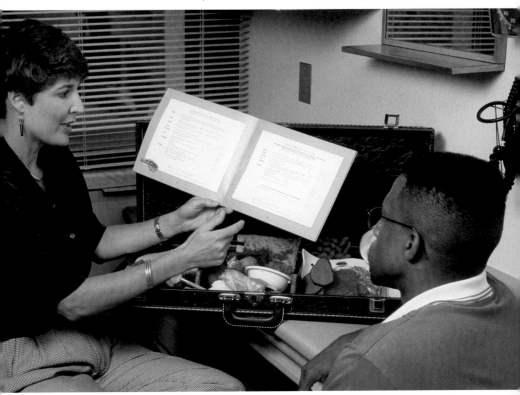

Treating Malnutrition by Educating People

In poor, undeveloped countries, alleviating malnutrition most often involves getting food to those who have none. In affluent countries, by contrast, sufficient food supplies are available, but people may not eat balanced diets and thereby become malnourished. The World Bank, an organization that assists needy people around the world, gives this advice about eliminating malnutrition in developing countries.

Many conditions of poor health are so common in developing countries that they are not recognized as abnormal. These may include mild and moderate malnutrition [as well as] anemia [and other medical conditions]. Often, a first step [in treating these disorders] is to make individuals and communities aware of these problems or of high-risk conditions that should be a cause of seeking services. In addition, mothers and/or communities may need their confidence and skills enhanced [through education by medical authorities] so that they feel that they themselves can take actions that will really make a difference.

World Bank, "Communication That Improves Nutrition." http://siteresources.worldbank.org/NUTRITION/Resources/Tool9-chap1.pdf.

Doctors and other caregivers have found that some patients respond better to group support than individual counseling. In a group setting, a counselor meets periodically with several people who share the same problem. By speaking openly with others who have similar food issues, the patient can learn how these other sufferers have managed to deal with their own problems. And that might inspire the patient to try these strategies in his or her own situation. Group sessions have also been known to help patients deal better with family and money problems, depression, alcohol and drug addiction, and other factors that frequently contribute to the onset of malnutrition.

In addition, group support can guide some patients toward more healthful cooking and eating habits.

Thus, a wide range of treatments is available to deal with malnutrition in affluent societies. In contrast, in poorer countries in which large segments of the population are hungry and malnourished, such treatments are often in short supply. One thing is certain: Whatever treatments may be available in a country, the doctors who administer them must be on the lookout for more than one kind of malnutrition. As it turns out, lack of food is not the only cause of the condition. Some people get plenty to eat, yet they are still malnourished.

CHAPTER FOUR

When Essential Nutrients Are Lacking

So far, the emphasis has been on examining what might be called the classic form of malnutrition, in which someone does not get enough to eat and as a result suffers weight loss, accompanied by other undesirable symptoms. However, this is by no means the only form of malnutrition that plagues humanity. In societies across the world, both affluent and poor, large numbers of people regularly suffer from other kinds of malnutrition in which the amount of food is not an issue. In fact, these individuals usually have plenty to eat. And in an unexpected twist, many of them are actually overweight rather than underweight.

Vitamin and Mineral Deficiencies

Some of these well-fed but still malnourished people are victims of what medical experts sometimes call micronutrient malnutrition. Micronutrients are substances, including vitamins and minerals, that the body requires in small amounts to maintain regular health. When a person fails to consume adequate amounts of a particular vitamin or mineral, he or she can acquire one of a group of serious illnesses associated with micronutrient malnutrition. Because these illnesses involve deficiencies of various vital nutrients, they are often referred to as deficiency diseases (or vitamin and mineral deficiencies).

Among the better-known deficiency diseases are scurvy, beriberi, pellagra, rickets, and iron-deficiency anemia.

Millions of people in countries where mass hunger exists also suffer from these ailments. If someone has inadequate supplies of food, he or she will almost certainly lack proper amounts of micronutrients. In more affluent countries, where food supplies are abundant, the problem is that many people do not eat balanced, nutritious diets. And they can become vitamin deficient and malnourished, quite often without realizing it. In fact, it is difficult, if not impossible, for medical authorities to determine just how many people are affected by micronutrient deficiencies.

Both the prevalence of such deficiencies in American society and the relative ease with which some of them can be cured is well illustrated by the case of folic acid. This vitamin is essential to reproduction and normal development of fetuses. One subtle but very damaging result of folic acid deficiency in mothers is the neural tube (developing spinal cord) disorder known as spina bifida. According to a recent PBS report:

> Spina bifida can [in many cases] actually be prevented in a developing fetus by the intake of folic acid. It's especially important that folic acid, found naturally in dark green leafy vegetables, strawberries, oranges, and beans, as well as in most multivitamins, is taken by a woman before she becomes pregnant as well as throughout her pregnancy. After 1998, when folic acid was added to cereals, breads, pastas, and other enriched or fortified grain products, the rate of neural tube disorders in the United States fell 26 percent within the next three years.[24]

Scurvy and Vitamin C

At first glance it might seem perplexing that it was not until the 1990s that the medical establishment and government made a serious attempt to address the problem of folic acid malnourishment in American society. But it must be kept in mind that scientists became aware of the existence and functions of vitamins and minerals only fairly recently. Between

1912 and 1918, Polish biochemist Casimir Funk, English biochemist Frederick G. Hopkins, and American biochemist
Elmer V. McCollum first isolated some of the major vitamins
and discovered how they contribute to proper nutrition.

Before the work of these pioneers, and indeed throughout
human history, large numbers of people regularly suffered
from micronutrient malnutrition but had no idea why or of
how to alleviate it. A major step in the right direction occurred
in the 1740s. Before that time it was extremely common for
sailors on long voyages to come down with a mysterious illness they came to call scurvy. After a few weeks at sea, the debilitating symptoms would begin to show themselves. The
sailors would grow weak, lose their appetite, experience joint
pain, and eventually suffer from numerous skin sores and
bleeding gums. If these sufferers stayed away from shore long
enough, most of them died. This scourge was so rampant that

The mouth of a person with scurvy, or vitamin C deficiency.

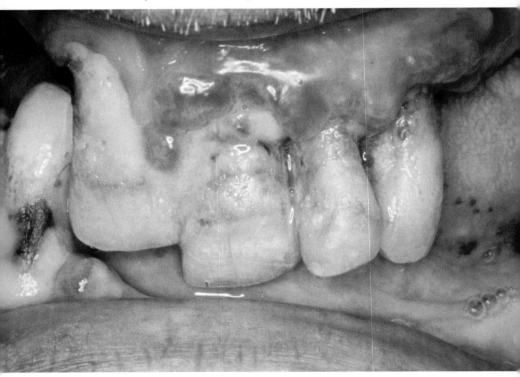

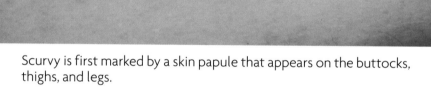

Scurvy is first marked by a skin papule that appears on the buttocks, thighs, and legs.

during the 1600s and early 1700s, more English sailors died of scurvy than perished in wars.

Hoping to end this suffering, a Scottish doctor named James Lind tackled the problem. After much study, he noted that most Dutch sailors did not contract scurvy, even on very long voyages. What were the Dutch sailors doing differently than seamen from other lands, Lind wondered? For one thing, he found that they regularly took along large supplies of fresh fruits on their voyages. This seemed to suggest that something in the fruit kept the men from getting the disease. To test his theory, in May 1747 Lind boarded a British ship, carrying with him large supplies of citrus fruits and green vegetables. "The results," nutritional expert John Heinerman writes,

> were truly astonishing and nothing short of a real miracle. Those [sailors who were] fed these foods didn't get scurvy.

James Lind discovered the link between vitamin C deficiency and scurvy.

And those who were given regular ship's fare to begin with got it, but then saw a total disappearance of their sufferings once they began eating the same vitamin-C-rich foods their companions had been subsisting on.[25]

At the time, of course, Lind did not know what it was in the fruits and vegetables that prevented the onset of scurvy. He had no inkling of the existence of vitamin C (ascorbic acid), nor did he realize that scurvy is a deficiency disease caused by inadequate amounts of vitamin C in the diet. At the time, though, his research was a breakthrough. In 1795 the British navy mandated that all its sailors receive doses of lemon or lime juice on long voyages; as a result, scurvy among English sailors virtually disappeared. Later, in 1932, American biochemist Charles G. King discovered vitamin C, and soon it became clear how this substance is essential in the manufacture of bones, teeth, tissues, and skin.

Today, scurvy is rare in developed countries like the United States, partly because many people get sufficient supplies of fruits and vegetables; also, numerous foods and vitamin supplements are fortified with vitamin C. A number of Americans still contract scurvy each year, however; most of them are elderly people and infants with inadequate diets. Scurvy affecting babies is usually referred to as Barlow's disease.

Beriberi and Pellagra

Another debilitating and sometimes fatal form of micronutrient malnutrition—beriberi—results from a lack of vitamin B1,

Trying to Find the Beriberi Culprit

Over the centuries, millions of people around the world suffered from beriberi but had no idea what caused the disease or how to avoid it. A major breakthrough came in 1882, when a Japanese doctor named Kanechiro Takaki suspected that diet was involved. He found a group of sailors suffering from beriberi and noted that their diet consisted almost exclusively of rice. When he fed them meat and vegetables, their symptoms disappeared. Takaki concluded that some substance that cured beriberi existed in vegetables but not in rice, but this turned out to be incorrect. The problem was that, like most Asians at that time, the sailors had eaten rice that had been polished, or had its outer husks removed. Once polished, the rice lacked the vitamin thiamine, which collects mainly in the husks. In 1897 a Dutch scientist, Christiaan Eijkman, performed an experiment that showed that animals and people who eat unpolished rice do not usually contract beriberi, which is caused by a thiamine deficiency. Eventually, other researchers isolated thiamine and explained its role in nutrition.

or thiamine, in the diet. Symptoms include fatigue, depression, constipation, nerve damage, muscle pain and/or paralysis, and heart problems. If left untreated, the sufferer usually dies.

Today, most cases of beriberi occur in poor countries where famine is widespread. However, a number of cases are reported each year in developed nations. Quite a few are mild and result from lower-than-normal intake of thiamine due to poor diet, while the more serious cases are most often seen among alcohol abusers who substitute alcohol for nutritious foods in their diet for extended periods. If properly diagnosed in its early stages, the disease can be successfully treated by getting the patient to eat more thiamine-rich foods. Among others, these include poultry, fish, beans, peas, and peanuts.

Fish, poultry, and green vegetables, along with dairy products and certain other foods, also contain stores of another important B vitamin, niacin. People who do not consume enough

The tongue of a patient with pellagra, caused by a niacin deficiency.

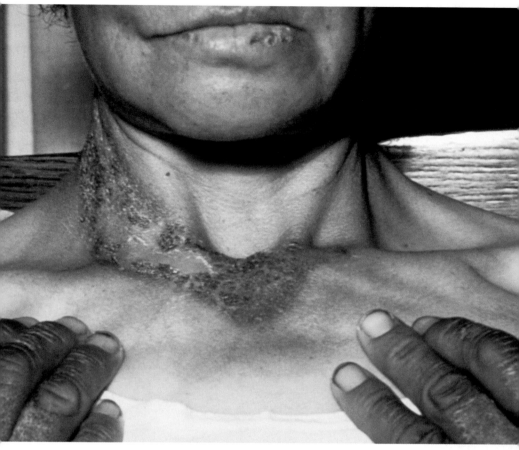

Pellagra results in thickening, peeling, and discoloration of the skin.

foods rich in niacin (or do not take vitamin pills containing it) can contract a deficiency disease known as pellagra. The initial symptoms include muscular weakness, indigestion, and skin sores. In more severe cases, the victim experiences dermatitis, a skin condition characterized by cracking and scaling, along with diarrhea, dementia (an emotional and mental disorder), and inflammation of the mucous membranes inside the mouth.

Once pellagra is diagnosed, mild cases can be successfully treated by making sure the patient eats fish, vegetables, and/or dairy products on a regular basis. People with severe cases are not so fortunate, however. The damage to their skin, which can be extensive, can result in permanent, unsightly scarring.

Vitamin D and Calcium Malnourishment

Fortunately, pellagra, scurvy, beriberi, and several other deficiency diseases are easily preventable. The vitamins with which they are associated exist in a wide range of foods, and all one has to do is make sure to eat a balanced diet. The same cannot be said, however, for another common form of micronutrient malnutrition: rickets. Rickets, which displays symptoms that include fragile bones and enlarged knees and

Rickets, which displays symptoms that include fragile bones and enlarged knees and other joints, is caused by a deficiency of vitamin D.

other joints, is caused by a deficiency of vitamin D. This substance is vital to metabolizing calcium, an important mineral needed for building and maintaining the bones and teeth.

The problem is that vitamin D exists naturally in fewer foods than any other vitamin. In fact, its main natural food source is fish-liver oil. The other main source of vitamin D is sunlight, which human skin absorbs and converts into the vitamin. Under normal circumstances, therefore, the chances of contracting rickets would be high for the many people who do not get much sun exposure and eat little or no fish. Fortunately, in the 1930s food manufacturers in developed countries began adding vitamin D to milk, bread, beer, and several other common food products. These supplements greatly reduced the incidence of rickets in the United States and in other industrialized nations. Still, some people, particularly strict vegetarians, remain at risk for vitamin D malnourishment and should take vitamin supplements that contain this crucial nutrient.

Partly because the functions of vitamin D and the mineral calcium are so closely interrelated, rickets can also be caused by a calcium deficiency. In addition, inadequate calcium in the diet can cause stunted growth and/or poorly developed bones and teeth in children as well as osteoporosis (brittle bones) in elderly people. U.S. health authorities estimate that as many as 10 million Americans suffer from osteoporosis and another 35 million are at risk for it at any given time. Thus, people of all ages need to be aware of the potential harm this very common form of malnutrition can cause. And they must be sure either to consume foods rich in calcium and vitamin D, or to take supplements containing these substances, or both.

Not Enough Iron

Although it is relatively easy to become deficient in vitamin D or calcium, U.S. health authorities report that the most common form of micronutrient malnutrition is iron deficiency. Abnormally low levels of the mineral iron are particularly common in newborn infants, especially premature babies. In addition, some studies indicate that between 5 and 7 percent of children aged four to eight in the United States suffer from a deficiency illness called iron deficiency anemia, which is an inadequate amount of iron in the blood. Likewise, as many as 35 to 55 percent of young women in the country suffer from some degree of anemia because of lack of iron in their diets. Percentages are even higher, for both women and men, in poorer, developing nations.

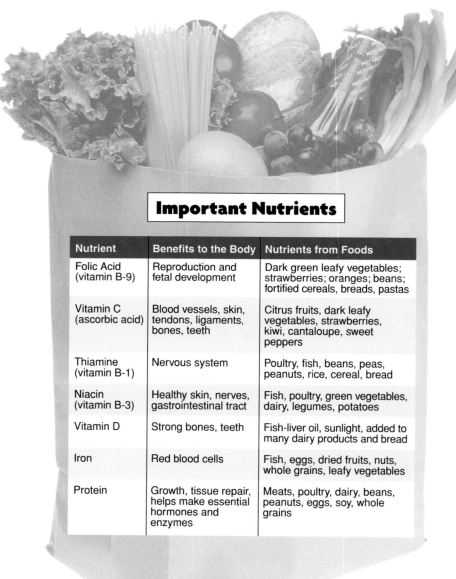

Important Nutrients

Nutrient	Benefits to the Body	Nutrients from Foods
Folic Acid (vitamin B-9)	Reproduction and fetal development	Dark green leafy vegetables; strawberries; oranges; beans; fortified cereals, breads, pastas
Vitamin C (ascorbic acid)	Blood vessels, skin, tendons, ligaments, bones, teeth	Citrus fruits, dark leafy vegetables, strawberries, kiwi, cantaloupe, sweet peppers
Thiamine (vitamin B-1)	Nervous system	Poultry, fish, beans, peas, peanuts, rice, cereal, bread
Niacin (vitamin B-3)	Healthy skin, nerves, gastrointestinal tract	Fish, poultry, green vegetables, dairy, legumes, potatoes
Vitamin D	Strong bones, teeth	Fish-liver oil, sunlight, added to many dairy products and bread
Iron	Red blood cells	Fish, eggs, dried fruits, nuts, whole grains, leafy vegetables
Protein	Growth, tissue repair, helps make essential hormones and enzymes	Meats, poultry, dairy, beans, peanuts, eggs, soy, whole grains

Prolonged periods of inadequate amounts of iron in the diet can lead to serious consequences. This mineral is absolutely essential to the creation of red blood cells, which carry oxygen to cells throughout the body, including those in the brain, the functions of which can be adversely affected by low levels of iron. "In recent years," Heinerman points out,

> medical researchers have found that iron deficiency is associated with the often irreversible impairment of a child's learning ability and other behavioral abnormalities. Low levels of this mineral can have a tremendous adverse impact on brain function. Besides this, diminished levels of iron in adults can affect how they work and what is accomplished, as well as increasing their chances of getting and dying from infection because of impaired immune defenses.[26]

Experts advise eating a diet rich in various foods containing iron, including fish, eggs, dried fruits, nuts, whole grains, and leafy vegetables, or, when necessary, taking an iron supplement.

Protein Malnutrition and Obesity

Whereas vitamins and minerals are usually referred to as micronutrients, protein is often called a macronutrient because people need much larger amounts of it to maintain health. For most people, the most familiar forms of macronutrient malnutrition are those associated with starvation, in which a person lacks sufficient foods of all kinds, including those containing protein. However, in affluent countries it is common to see another, equally unhealthy kind of macronutrient malnutrition. In short, over the course of months, and sometimes years, some poeple eat predominantly starchy, sugary, and fatty foods containing little protein. Because such people get plenty to eat and the foods they consume are high in calories, they either maintain or gain weight. Some eat so much food that they become obese (that is, they increase their normal body weight by 20 to 30 percent or more); yet they are still malnourished. The problem, therefore, is not the amount of food they eat but rather the lack of proper nutrients in that food.

Factors Promoting Obesity

This excerpt from a recent PBS report lists some of the social and environmental factors that have contributed to the rise of obesity caused by macronutrient malnutrition in recent years.

Environment plays a major role in obesity. Urbanization means most jobs are nearly free of hard physical labor, and more and more frequently, people rely on driving and not walking as their main means of transportation. Advertising promotes high-calorie and low-nutrient food and drink. Snack machines in schools and offices are a popular destination in busy lives, and restaurants typically offer "super-size" portions. Heavy intake of sugar and corn syrup, coupled with a sedentary lifestyle, are major contributing factors to Americans' current high incidence of obesity. Americans consume an average of 128 pounds of sugar per person, up 27 pounds since the 1970s.

PBS, "Deadly Diseases: Malnutrition." www.pbs.org/wgbh/rxforsurvival/series/diseases/malnutrition.html.

Many factors contribute to the growing incidence of this form of malnutrition in the United States and other affluent countries. According to the organization Bread for the World, some of these factors are economic and others behavioral:

> Low income people may consume greater amounts of less expensive, high-calorie and high-fat foods to guard against hunger, or may be unable to afford sufficient amounts of more nutritious food. Cash-strapped families may increasingly rely on fast food chains, which promote "value" meals, such as oversized burgers, extra-large servings of fries and buckets of soda. Healthier foods, such as meat, fish, fresh fruits, vegetables and whole grains, often are more expensive than alternative junk food. Poor neighborhoods often lack large grocery stores that typically offer the lowest prices and greatest range of brands,

package sizes and quality choices. . . . Consequently, many families in low-income neighborhoods depend on their corner convenience stores, which often are stocked with high-cost, processed, pre-packaged foods. [27]

Yet lower-income people are not the only ones who suffer from obesity. People in all income brackets and of all ages are constantly bombarded by advertising that promotes fatty, sugary foods that have little nutritional value. And the majority of people do not get enough physical activity and exercise. As a result, according to the U.S. National Center for Health Statistics, in 2006 about 30 percent of Americans aged twenty or older, amounting to some 60 million people, were obese. Incredibly, these figures have tripled since 1980, indicating an alarming trend. Obese people run higher-than-normal risks of developing high blood pressure, diabetes, sleep apnea, stroke, heart disease, and other debilitating problems.

Doctors and other health experts say that the key to avoiding obesity and its harmful effects is twofold. First, people should educate themselves, their children, and others about the dangers of macronutrient (as well as micronutrient) malnutrition and about what constitutes a healthy diet. Second, they should adjust their eating habits accordingly and get plenty of exercise. Fortunately, given time and individual dedication and perseverance, obesity, along with most nutrient deficiencies, can be overcome.

CHAPTER FIVE

Intentional Malnutrition: Eating Disorders

Mass starvation in poor countries, poor nutrition in affluent nations, and deficiencies caused by illness in all countries have one thing in common; namely, none of the malnourished people involved purposely sets out to deny his or her body proper nutrition. None of them consciously adopts a personal strategy of self-starvation or of purging food they have already eaten.

These kinds of self-destructive acts are associated with still another cause of malnutrition—eating disorders. Eating disorders are physical-psychological conditions in which the sufferer abuses food, causing illness, and/or a malnourished state, and/or disruptive and sometimes life-threatening lifestyle changes. The American Psychiatric Association and other leading medical organizations in the United States and around the world recognize several different eating disorders. Two, however, are particularly relevant to the issue of malnutrition—anorexia nervosa and bulimia.

What Are Anorexia and Bulimia?

The term *anorexia* has become more or less synonymous with the act of self-starvation. Anorexic individuals (often referred to simply as anorexics) typically eat very little on a daily basis and over time become extremely thin. According to the Eating Disorder Referral and Information Center:

> Individuals with anorexia nervosa are unwilling or unable to maintain a body weight that is normal or expectable for their age and height. (Most clinicians use 85% of normal weight as a guide.) Individuals with anorexia nervosa typically display a pronounced fear of weight gain and a dread of becoming fat although they are dramatically underweight. Concerns and perceptions about their weight have an extremely powerful influence and impact on their self-evaluation. The seriousness of the weight loss and its physical effects is minimized or denied. (Women with the diagnosis of anorexia nervosa have missed at least three consecutive menstrual cycles.)[28]

If left untreated, the disorder can cause severe physical harm and even death. Studies conducted since the 1980s indicate that approximately 10 percent of anorexics eventually die, while nearly all run a high risk of suffering debilitating bodily damage and disabling emotional disturbances.

The other eating disorder that frequently causes malnutrition is bulimia. Bulimic individuals (or bulimics) typically engage in cycles of what medical experts call bingeing and purging. That is, bulimics eat very large amounts of food in one sitting and then almost immediately afterward get rid of it by vomiting or other means (such as laxatives). At first glance, the fact that anorexics eat very little and bulimics eat a great deal might give the impression that the two disorders are quite different. In reality, however, they are closely related. Most anorexics begin as bulimics or else alternate periods of starvation with periods of bingeing and purging. Also, both disorders have the same underlying causes, share many symptoms, and usually lead to a state of malnutrition.

Anorexia and bulimia are seen mainly in developed, affluent countries, including the United States. The U.S. National Institute of Mental Health estimates that between 1 and 4 percent of adolescent and adult women in Western nations suffer

Who Is at Risk for Eating Disorders?

Kathryn J. Zerbe, an eating disorders specialist at the Menninger Clinic in Topeka, Kansas, describes the social groups most at risk for developing anorexia and bulimia.

Traditionally, most victims of eating disorders have been thought to be white, economically well-off girls or young women. This remains largely true, although the picture does seems to be changing. Recent studies have shown that growing numbers of African-Americans and other minorities are becoming afflicted with eating disorders, especially bulimia. Boys and men are also at increasing risk for eating disorders. Although studies show that nine out of ten victims are female, males who participate in certain sports (e.g., wrestling, gymnastics, running), are homosexual, or who suffer from addiction or personal disorders are at greater risk of developing an eating disorder. Anorexic males can be just as preoccupied with body image as females, but tend to want to have a slender waist and muscular, athletic shoulders and chest. This is sometimes called "reverse anorexia."

Eating disorders are appearing among all socioeconomic groups. They are crossing age barriers, showing up in younger and younger children. More and more preschool and grade schoolers are developing eating problems, showing preoccupation with weight and size, and going on diets.

Kathryn J. Zerbe, "A Body to Die For: The ABCs of Eating Disorders." www.thedoctor willseeyounow.com/articles/behavior/eatdis_8.

from anorexia. (Only 5 to 15 percent of anorexics are male.) And at least twice as many people, both female and male, are bulimic (although again women outnumber men). That means that as many as 8 to 10 million people may be anorexic and 16 to 20 million may be bulimic in the United States alone.

Bulimia: Symptoms and Effects

These figures may seem surprising, even shocking to some, partly because people with eating disorders often do not tell anyone about their eating problems. Bulimics, for example, frequently try to hide their condition. Typical behavior is to make a trip to the bathroom following a meal, lock the door, purge into the toilet, flush, and thereafter keep this activity secret from family and friends. In the beginning, the sufferer may lose little or no weight and act and appear normal. It is not unusual, therefore, for a brother to be unaware that his sister is bulimic or even for a husband not to realize that his wife suffers from the condition.

Bulimia is an eating disorder characterized by eating great amounts of food and then almost immediately throwing up.

Eventually, however, certain symptoms of bulimia can begin to become apparent, particularly when family and friends know what to look for. First, the repeated vomiting associated with the disorder causes stomach acids to damage the esophagus, throat, gums, and teeth. Over time the acid can actually eat away the enamel protecting the teeth and cause the jaw to swell. The constant vomiting also stresses the stomach, causing abdominal pain. In addition, most bulimics feel ashamed of what they are doing, including lying to loved ones, and the result can be depression and general feelings of unhappiness. This range of symptoms can be difficult to hide from relatives and friends, as in the case of a teenaged bulimic named Ann, who later admitted:

> I lived in terror that my parents and brother would find out [about my bingeing and purging]. I constantly lied about what I was doing. When I was sixteen, I started getting really bad stomach cramps and sore throats. I had trouble getting to sleep at night. . . . I wanted to ask my parents for help, but was afraid they'd completely freak out. So I got very depressed. I couldn't concentrate on anything and I started getting bad grades in school. . . . Eventually, I couldn't face it any more. When I was seventeen I tried slitting my wrists. It didn't work, but that's when everybody found out.[29]

In addition to these adverse physical and emotional effects and family strife, chronic bulimics have a high risk of becoming malnourished. They may suffer from one or more micronutrient deficiencies or not get enough protein. Moreover, having come to view food as a sort of enemy, they may begin to transition into anorexic behavior, which can lead to abnormal weight loss and a more serious case of malnutrition.

Anorexia: Symptoms and Effects

Like bulimics, anorexics have an intense fear of becoming fat and react by rejecting food. But whereas a bulimic rejects food by first eating it and then throwing it up, an anorexic does so by refusing to eat in the first place. Medical authorities esti-

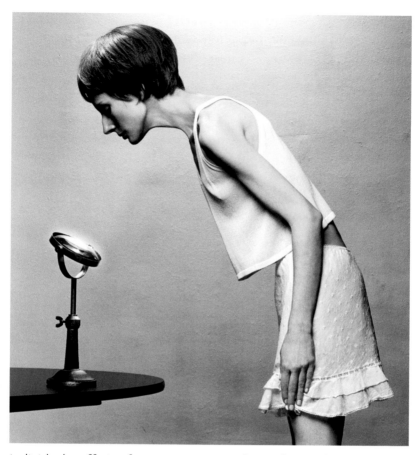

Individuals suffering from anorexia view themselves as fat, even when they are very, very thin.

mate that a typical anorexic person eats and keeps down only two hundred to five hundred food calories per day; that is only about a fifth or less of what a normal, healthy person eats.

Not surprisingly, such self-starvation will inevitably lead to some or many of the same symptoms and harmful effects associated with the types of malnutrition caused by mass hunger and illness. "Physical signs and symptoms," says one leading eating disorders watchdog group,

> include, but are not limited to, constipation, abnormally low heart rate, abdominal distress, dryness of skin, hypertension, fine body hair, [and] lack of menstrual periods.

Anorexia nervosa causes anemia, cardiovascular [heart] problems, changes in brain structure, osteoporosis, and kidney dysfunction.[30]

In addition to these physical symptoms and effects, chronic anorexics often suffer mental depression and disruptive changes in normal activities, lifestyle, and personal and social relationships. According to authorities on the disorder, the act of self-starvation eventually brings on feelings of fatigue and changes in temperament. "There is simply not enough energy available to keep up normal life as it was known before," Grainne Smith, an expert on anorexia, explains.

> Even talking takes energy, and often friends are dropped as social life is curtailed, quite apart from the fact that [an anorexic] finds it impossible to believe that anyone could love her or have an interest in her. [The anorexic] begins to sound irritable and bad-tempered over trivial things that never caused a problem before, and her perceptions of relationships and events change and distort as she loses the ability to think clearly and logically.[31]

The Causes of Eating Disorders

It is possible that some people suffered from these physical and mental effects of anorexia and bulimia in past generations, but if so, no one knows how many did so and for how long. The fact is that doctors and other medical authorities did not become widely aware of these disorders and begin to study, understand, and treat them in any meaningful way until the 1970s and 1980s. Major public awareness of these problems first came in 1982 with the publication of the book *Starving for Attention* by Cherry Boone O'Neill, daughter of singer and actor Pat Boone. In this best seller, the author details her painful ordeals with both bulimia and anorexia. Less than a year later, the popular singer Karen Carpenter (of the group the Carpenters) died of heart failure caused by long-term anorexia.

Doctors naturally wanted to know what caused these cases of self-inflicted malnutrition as well as the rapidly growing number of other reported cases of anorexia and bulimia. It soon became clear that there is no single primary cause. Rather, many and diverse factors often combine to induce these disorders, and because the combination of factors can vary from person to person, no two cases are ever exactly alike. According to the National Eating Disorders Association, these factors can include low self-esteem, feelings of inadequacy or lack of control of one's own life, depression and/or loneliness, family problems, and a history of sexual abuse or frequent ridicule of one's weight or body size.

Pop singer Karen Carpenter was one of the first celebrities to bring the public's attention to eating disorders.

Experts on eating disorders also point out another important contributing factor to the development of anorexia and bulimia—pervasive cultural pressures that glorify thinness. According to this view, the media, clothing designers and manufacturers, and advertisers of a wide range of products regularly portray thin people, especially thin women, as the most desirable, virtuous, successful, and happy people. On the one hand, this has spawned a widespread obsession with fad diets, most of which do not work and end with the dieter regaining all the lost weight, often plus some extra. On the other, it has painted overweight people and sometimes even those of normal weight, as having no willpower or as being unglamorous. This can lead some people, including many young women, to strive overly hard to be thin.

"Reality Retreats"

Adding to and complicating these factors is another that is closely associated with eating disorders—poor or distorted body image. Even when an anorexic is abnormally thin, even skeletal looking, Smith points out, she (or he) will typically argue that

> she is in fact quite gross. [The anorexic's] view in the mirror, in front of which she spends much anxious time, is distorted. Where others see bones standing out through clothes, she sees fat. Where others see hollows, she sees roundness. And [this] drives [her] on to even greater efforts in self-starvation. Reality retreats as anorexia takes over. . . . Both [bulimics] and [anorexics] think that no one could possibly love someone so fat, so gross, so lacking in self-discipline.[32]

It is also possible that these psychological and social causes of eating disorders are compounded by physical or genetic factors. But if so, the role played by these factors is not yet well understood. The National Eating Disorders Association reports:

> Scientists are still researching possible biochemical or biological causes of eating disorders. In some individuals

with eating disorders, certain chemicals in the brain that control hunger, appetite, and digestion have been found to be imbalanced. The exact meaning and implications of these imbalances remains under investigation.[33]

Treating Eating Disorders

Treatment of eating disorders is often more difficult than simply treating the symptoms of the malnutrition these disorders produce. In the case of a poor person who cannot find enough to eat or that of a sick person who has temporarily lost his or her appetite, the denial of nutrition is not intentional. Most often, these sorts of malnourished individuals are happy to resume normal eating habits when and if possible. Anorexics and bulimics, by contrast, do not desire to eat (or to keep the food down), usually because of complex and deep-seated emotional and psychological reasons. So doctors and other health-care professionals must address the patient's emotional and psychological issues as well as his or her physical symptoms.

As for treating the physical symptoms of eating disorders, the chief goal is to get the person to eat a healthy diet and, if necessary, gain some weight. This can be difficult in cases in which a person has been bulimic and/or anorexic for a long time. He or she may at first pretend to go along with the treatment. But when the caregiver's back is turned, the person might sneak into the bathroom and vomit, reinforcing old, harmful habits. Sometimes, therefore, the patient needs constant monitoring, at least until he or she can be trusted. For anorexics who are dangerously thin and suffering from a wide range of adverse symptoms, a period of hospitalization, including forced feeding via feeding tubes, is sometimes necessary.

Drug therapy is also sometimes used to treat eating disorders. Antidepressants are frequently prescribed because they can partially or fully lift the patient's depression, which is a major contributing cause of anorexia and bulimia. Yet results have been mixed. Some doctors say that they have had considerable success in treating anorexics with antidepressants; others report little or no success. All seem to agree, however, that these substances are effective in treating bulimia.

Recovery Rates for Eating Disorders

The noted information outlet Anorexia Nervosa and Related Eating Disorders gives these statistics about the success rates of treating anorexia and bulimia.

With treatment, about sixty percent (60%) of people with eating disorders recover. They maintain healthy weight, eat a varied diet of normal foods . . . participate in friendships and romantic relationships, and create families and careers. Many say they feel they are stronger people and more insightful about life in general and themselves in particular than they would have been without the disorder. In spite of treatment, about twenty percent (20%) of people with eating disorders make only partial recoveries. They remain too much focused on food and weight, participate only superficially in friendships and romantic relationships, and may hold jobs but seldom have meaningful careers. Much of each paycheck goes to diet books, laxatives, jazzercise classes, and binge food. The remaining twenty percent (20%) do not improve, even with treatment. They are seen repeatedly in emergency rooms, eating disorders programs, and mental health clinics. Their quietly desperate lives revolve around food and weight concerns, spiraling down into depression, loneliness, and feelings of helplessness and hopelessness.

Anorexia Nervosa and Related Eating Disorders, "How Many People Have Eating Disorders?" www.anred.com/stats.html.

Whatever medicines may be prescribed, drug therapy is never used by itself to treat eating disorders. Instead, it is employed as a supplement to psychological treatment, one version of which consists of a doctor teaching the patient slowly to improve his or her eating habits. Good behaviors are reinforced with rewards, such as allowing the patient to participate in certain social activities or to have extra time alone, without a monitor. Counseling therapy is also used. Over time, a trained therapist educates the patient about the causes of his or her problem and helps the person learn to deal with it emotionally.

It is important to emphasize that recovery for longtime anorexia or bulimia sufferers is often itself long and difficult. As Smith aptly puts it:

> Prepare for a long road. The average duration of [treatment for] anorexia nervosa is 5-7 years, with many setbacks. Some sufferers recover more quickly than others, but unfortunately sometimes the illness becomes chronic. . . . The sooner [anorexia] is recognized and treatment accepted the better the potential outcome. Two steps forward, one back; five forward, then five back . . . is a common pattern.[34]

Thus, the disturbing and sobering realities of eating disorders and the difficulty in treating them constitute still another demonstration of how malnutrition, in its diverse forms, is the most widespread debilitating medical condition in the world.

CHAPTER SIX

World Hunger: Crisis and Solutions

Although illness, ignorance about proper nutrition, eating disorders, and other factors cause a fair amount of malnutrition in affluent nations, the numbers of malnourished people in these places pale in comparison to the numbers in the world's poorest countries. Indeed, world hunger has long been and remains one of the worst crises facing humanity. Some experts think that the estimated figure of 850 million undernourished people worldwide may be too low. They suggest that the real number may be more than a billion, perhaps a full sixth of the planet's approximately 6.5 billion people. It is certainly beyond dispute that some 24,000 people die every day from malnutrition or causes related to it.

Overall, a majority of these victims of malnutrition are concentrated in poor, developing nations. For example, the United Nations (UN) estimates that in 2005 (the most recent year for which accurate figures are available) 43 million people in Bangladesh (nearly a third of the country's population) did not get enough to eat and were moderately to grossly undernourished. Some 31 million people were in similar circumstances in Ethiopia, 14 million in Indonesia, 11 million in Nigeria, 9 million in Sudan, and 8 million in North Korea. Of the continents, Africa had the highest number, having sixteen of the eighteen poorest and most malnourished nations.

It is revealing, however, that a large portion of the world's malnourished people dwell in countries that are industrialized and developed, or almost so. Some 212 million people were malnourished in India in 2005, for example. And about 150 million did not get enough to eat in China, while 35 million suffered the same fate in Pakistan.

Even the United States, the world's most affluent country, is not immune to the problem. An estimated 30 million Americans

The majority of malnutrition victims are concentrated in poor, developing nations. Sixteen of the eighteen poorest and most malnourished nations are in Africa.

fall under the designation *food insecure,* meaning they are often not sure where they will find their next meal. Some 12 million of these individuals are children. "If any other rapidly spreading epidemic was weakening the health, minds, and spirits of . . . 12 million children," noted journalist Loretta Schwartz-Nobel writes,

> there would be headlines in every major newspaper about it every day. But hunger is America's silent and hidden disease . . . [and] still remains largely unacknowledged at the highest political levels. Our leaders often speak of poverty, but "hunger" is a word that is almost never publicly mentioned.[35]

The Developed vs. the Developing World

International health-care experts and government officials point out that malnutrition produced by large-scale hunger and incidents of mass starvation exists mainly in the developing world. Overall, they say, it is more a matter of money than anything else that determines which nations suffer the most from hunger and malnutrition. Simply put, those countries whose governments and citizenry are the poorest suffer the most. According to figures released by the United Nations (UN), Bread for the World, and other international organizations, about fifty-seven countries make up the so-called developed world, with a combined population of some .9 billion people, roughly one-sixth of the global population. The other more than 5 billion people dwell in the developing world, composed of about 125 low- to middle-income nations, where the standard of living is significantly lower than in developed countries. The overall goal of UN and private relief efforts is to eliminate most or all occurrences of malnutrition in both the developed and developing worlds.

Global Malnutrition and Children

Schwartz-Nobel and other observers and experts often single out the dilemma of children in the global malnutrition crisis. This is partly because it is only natural for adults to be concerned about children's suffering and want to alleviate it. But there is also the fact that the world's children represent its future.

The huge scope of the problem of child malnutrition has been well documented by various UN agencies and private relief and charitable organizations. They have found that nearly 30 percent of children under age five in developing countries are unhealthily underweight. About 10 percent—in sheer numbers, tens of millions of them—are moderately to severely stunted, or considerably below the normal height for their age group.

Moreover, each year almost 11 million children under age five die from malnutrition-related causes. About three quarters of these tragic deaths take place in sub-Saharan Africa and south Asia, the two general areas that consistently have the highest rates of hunger and malnutrition. "Most of these deaths are attributed not to outright starvation," the humanitarian organization Bread for the World points out,

> but to diseases that move in on vulnerable children whose bodies have been weakened by hunger. Every year, more than 20 million low-birth weight babies are born in developing countries. These babies risk dying in infancy, while those who survive often suffer lifelong physical and cognitive disabilities. The four most common childhood illnesses are diarrhea, acute respiratory illness, malaria, and measles. Each of these illnesses is both preventable and treatable. Yet, again, poverty interferes in parents' ability to access immunizations and medicines. Chronic undernourishment on top of insufficient treatment greatly increases a child's risk of death.[36]

Why So Much Hunger and Malnutrition?

The reasons for this veritable epidemic of malnutrition in children, as well as in adults, across the globe are no mystery and have been written about extensively for the past two genera-tions. Perhaps not surprisingly, the single biggest cause is grind-ing poverty. In the United States, families are usually considered to be poor if they earn below a certain amount per year. According to the official U.S. poverty guidelines for 2006, a family of four that earns less than twenty thousand dollars per year is living in poverty. That amounts to about fifty-eight dollars per day. In many countries, however, such a family would be viewed as well-off; the international poverty line is much lower—a mere one dollar per day earned by a family breadwinner. The UN estimates that more than a billion people worldwide live in families that earn less than a dollar per day.

Many other factors besides poverty contribute to the high numbers of malnourished people in the world at any given time. First, drought and other natural disasters regularly take a heavy toll on the lives of people of lower-than-average in-come. For example, a severe drought ravaged the east African nation of Kenya between 2003 and 2006. (Actually, drought

A man near the ruins of his home in the tsunami-hit city of Banda Aceh, Indonesia, January 2005.

conditions began there in 1999 and were only temporarily alleviated by a single period of rain early in 2003.) More than 3 million Kenyans suffered from various effects of malnutrition in that period. And at least $250 million per year were required (and provided by the UN and private charities) simply to keep these people from starving to death. The enormous numbers of people who became homeless and hungry in the wake of the terrible December 2004 tsunami in the Indian Ocean region constitutes another example.

War, Ignorance, and Corruption

War, including conventional conflicts, civil wars, and efforts to commit genocide (wipe out an entire race or group), also accounts for a hefty proportion of world hunger and malnutrition. This has been particularly evident in recent years in Africa. Civil conflicts between 1983 and 2005 in the Sudan in northeastern Africa and genocidal policies in that same nation between 2004 and 2006 adversely affected the lives of at least 3.6 million poor people. A large proportion of these Sudanese, including an estimated 1.8 million children, were homeless at one point or another and suffered from varying degrees of malnutrition. Similarly, ethnic strife and civil war in the Democratic Republic of Congo in central Africa between 1997 and 2006 killed some 3.3 million people, most of whom died of malnutrition rather than from violence.

Many other cases of mass starvation have resulted from ignorance, neglect, and/or governmental corruption. For instance, poor land use has been common in various parts of Africa and Asia in the past century. Some farmers unknowingly exhausted the nutrients in their soil, and others tried (or were forced) to farm in areas where the soil could not support large-scale agriculture. Governments often ignored the plight of these rural poor. Even worse, in numerous instances corrupt government officials actually diverted and pocketed money and supplies that the UN and outside charities had intended to relieve the poor and starving.

Still another factor contributing to large-scale hunger and malnutrition in the world's poorer countries is the lack of a societal safety net in these countries. As a spokesman for one of the major relief organizations puts it:

> Countries in which a large portion of the population bat-
> tles hunger daily are usually poor and often lack the social
> safety nets we enjoy, such as soup kitchens, food stamps,
> and job training programs. When a family that lives in a
> poor country cannot grow enough food or earn enough
> money to buy food, there is nowhere to turn for help.[37]

Efforts to Fight World Hunger

Large-scale efforts to alleviate this perpetually reoccurring crisis of world hunger have been ongoing since the end of World
War II in the mid-1940s. Aid has generally consisted of two general kinds: first, international and government-based aid, and
second, private aid, including donations from charities and
wealthy individuals and fund-raising drives among ordinary
citizens. Chief among the international efforts have been those
of the United Nations, through several of its humanitarian
agencies, including the UN Children's Fund (UNICEF) and the
UN Food and Agricultural Organization (FAO). Some of these
efforts have concentrated on direct food shipments to famine-
ravaged regions. Another approach has been to send UN and
other international advisers into poverty-stricken areas to
teach farmers how to work their lands more efficiently and
grow more food. The UN has also tried, and at times suc-
ceeded, in brokering peace between local warring factions,
thereby allowing refugees and other displaced people to re-
turn to their homes and farms. Still another way the UN has
helped is by convincing the well-off members of the international community to forgive debts owed to them by impover-
ished nations in Africa and elsewhere.

Although each of these efforts achieved some measure of
success in the second half of the twentieth century, large-scale
hunger and malnutrition were far from eradicated. This
prompted a renewed effort by the UN beginning in the year
2000. That year a new, broad-based program called the UN Mil-
lennium Development Goals (MDGs) was launched, address-

Some Progress Made in Fighting Malnutrition

In 2006 UNICEF, one of the chief relief organizations of the United Nations, made this hopeful statement about recent progress made in the battle against global hunger and malnutrition.

The good news is that child malnutrition rates in the developing world fell from 32 per cent to 28 per cent during the 1990s, with 8 developing nations reducing malnutrition levels by 25 per cent or more. These include Bangladesh, China, Indonesia, Mexico and Vietnam. . . . [Progress was also made toward] the goal of eliminating vitamin A and iodine deficiencies. . . . The number of households in the developing world consuming iodized salt [which provides needed dietary iodine] has risen from less than 20 per cent in 1990 to over 70 per cent today. Half of the world's children are receiving vitamin A supplements, saving an estimated 300,000 lives each year.

UNICEF, "Nutrition: What Are the Challenges?" www.unicef.org/nutrition/index_chal lenges.html.

ing not only hunger but also many other social and economic ills plaguing the human community. The number-one goal on the list, however, is hunger-related. The aim is to reduce by at least one-half the number of people in the world living on less than a dollar per day and to reduce by at least one-half the number of people who suffer from hunger and malnutrition— all by the year 2015.

Those running the MDGs program say that putting these goals at the top of the list was not an arbitrary decision. They openly acknowledge that many of the other serious global social and economic problems they want to attack are always made worse by severe poverty and malnutrition. As Jacques Diouf, the director general of the FAO, points out, "We stand very little chance of achieving the rest of the goals [in the MDGs program]—environment, education, child mortality, maternal health, gender equality, HIV/AIDS—unless the first MDG [ending poverty and hunger] is achieved."[38]

A large part of the burden of the first goal in the MDGs program falls on the UN's World Food Programme (WFP), the world's largest humanitarian agency, with its headquarters in Rome, Italy. In 2005 alone, the WFP distributed 4.6 million tons (4.2 million metric tons) of food to 96.7 million people in

A Food Basket for the World's Hungry

The World Food Programme provides rations of 2,100,000 calories (2,100 kilocalories) to people worldwide every day.

Many of the world's hungry receive the following daily rations from the World Food Programme.

Rice / Wheat / Maize
14.11 ounces
(400 grams)

Beans
2.12 ounces
(60 grams)

Corn-soya blend
1.76 ounces
(50 grams)

Vegetable oil
.88 ounces
(25 grams)

Iodized salt
.18 ounces
(5 grams)

Sugar
.53 ounces
(15 grams)

United Nations World Food Programme, www.wfp.org/operations/introduction/relief_operations.asp?section=5&sub_section=1.

eighty-two countries. The WFP spent about $2.9 billion on these relief efforts in that year. The largest single portion of the relief went to food and medical aid for some 3.4 million hungry refugees in the Darfur region of the Sudan. Overall in 2005, the WFP helped roughly 58 million children, 30 percent of whom were under five, including the operation of programs that provided breakfasts and lunches in schools in seventy-four countries.

Private Donations and Initiatives

Much of the money needed to run the WFP's operations and other UN food and poverty programs comes from UN member nations, especially from well-off countries such as the United States, the United Kingdom, France, Germany, and others. However, a hefty portion of these funds comes from donations from private corporations and wealthy philanthropists (individuals who give away part of their fortunes to help charities and other worthy causes).

Up until 2006, the vast majority of these private donations amounted to a few million dollars, and on occasion in the tens of millions. It therefore made headlines around the globe when the richest man in the world made a stunning announcement that year. Bill Gates, chairman of the Microsoft Corporation, revealed the launching of a new global initiative to fight world hunger, one of truly enormous scope. Working in an alliance he had recently forged with the Rockefeller Foundation, Gates pledged $30 billion, a substantial portion of his vast fortune, to fighting poverty in underprivileged nations. Gates acknowledged that hunger and malnutrition could not be alleviated in any meaningful way without dealing with the underlying problem of abject poverty. "We've been looking into the causes of extreme poverty and how we might make a contribution to reducing that," he told reporters.

> If we can work on health and poverty issues concurrently, there is a lot that can be done to improve the quality of life. . . . Today no country of any size has been able to sustain a transition out of poverty without substantially raising

In 2006 Microsoft chairman Bill Gates and his wife Melinda pledged $30 billion to fight poverty in underprivileged nations.

productivity in the agricultural sector. It can have a transformative impact.[39]

Thus, although some of the money in the Gates/Rockefeller initiative will go toward providing food for those in immediate need, even more will be spent to raise the poorest people out of poverty and educate them about the most efficient means of growing food. The hope is that thereafter they will be self-sufficient and thereby have access to adequate food supplies. Africa's poorest regions will be targeted first, and other needy areas will be aided later. The initial goals of the project, according to the Web site of Gates's foundation, will be:

1. Breeding better crops that are adapted to the variety of local conditions in Africa. The goal is to develop 100 new varieties in five years.

2. Training African breeders and agricultural scientists who can spearhead this process in the future.

3. Guaranteeing reliable ways to get high-quality, locally adapted seeds into the hands of small farmers, through seed companies, public organizations, and a network of 10,000 agro-dealers, the small merchants largely responsible for providing supplies and knowledge to Africa's farmers.[40]

Inspired in part by Gates's generosity, another famous billionaire, Warren Buffett, joined the same effort, pledging more than $30 billion of his own money to fight global poverty and hunger.

Thus, the fight against world hunger and the crippling effects of large-scale malnutrition is being waged on many fronts by many caring and dedicated people. More money than ever before has been pledged to this gargantuan battle, giving many of those involved in the effort hope that it can inevitably be won. As for whether the scourge of world hunger can or will be eradicated in the foreseeable future, only time will tell. What is more certain is that neither national governments, nor health-care professionals, nor ordinary individuals can afford to ignore the ever-present threat of malnutrition.

Notes

Introduction: A Global Problem with Many Faces

1. World Health Organization, "Malnutrition Worldwide." www.mikeschoice.com/reports/malnutrition_world wide.htm.
2. Ramzi R. Hajjar et al., "Malnutrition in Aging." www.ispub.com/ostia/index.php?xmlFilePath=journals/ijgg/vol1n1/malnutrition.xml.
3. The study was conducted by the Commonwealth Fund in New York City, a private organization that investigates and works to improve health care in the United States.
4. Quoted in UNICEF, "The State of the World's Children—UNICEF 1998 Report," 1998. www.isleofavalon.co.uk/GlastonburyArchive/manymany/issue-66/mm-66g.html.

Chapter 1: The Kinds and Causes of Malnutrition

5. Quoted in Donna G. Grigsby, "Malnutrition." www.emedi cine.com/ PED/topic1360.htm.
6. Grigsby, "Malnutrition."
7. Cesar Chelala, "Child Hunger in a Land of Abundance Makes Us All Poor," *Philadelphia Inquirer*, September 24, 2006. www.bread.org/press-room/news/page.jsp?item ID=30339775.
8. National Institute on Alcohol Abuse and Alcoholism, "Alcohol and Your Health." www.healthchecksystems. com/alcohol.htm.
9. Joel B. Mason, "Malnutrition and the Cancer Patient." www.thedoctorwillseeyounow.com/articles/nutrition/malnucancer_15.

10. American Liver Foundation, "Diet and Your Liver." www.liverfoundation.org/db/articles/1022.

11. National Institute of Mental Health, "Depression." www.nimh.nih.gov/publicat/depression.cfm.

12. Staff of the Mayo Clinic, "Malnutrition and Seniors: When a Relative Doesn't Eat Enough." www.mayoclinic.com/health/senior-health/HA00066.

Chapter 2: Recognizing the Symptoms of Malnutrition

13. Lab Tests Online, "Malnutrition." www.labtestsonline.org/understanding/conditions/malnutrition-2.html.

14. Alisha Durtschi, "Determining Deficiency Diseases Caused by Malnutrition." http://waltonfeed.com/self/health/vit-min/summary.html. Based on Appendix 28 in L. Kathleen Mahan, ed., *Krause's Food, Nutrition, and Diet Therapy*. Philadelphia: W.B. Saunders, 1996.

15. Quoted in Janet Walzer, "Growth Interrupted: Two Countries Work Together to Reduce Stunting in Peruvian Children." http://nutrition.tufts.edu/magazine/2003 fall/peru.html.

16. World Resources Institute, "Malnutrition." http://pubs.wri.org/pubs_content_text.cfm?ContentID=1365.

17. Douglas MacKay and Alan L. Miller, "Nutritional Support for Wound Healing," *Alternative Medical Review*, vol. 8, 2003, pp. 360–61.

18. Doctors Without Borders, "Acute Malnutrition." www.doctorswithoutborders.org/news/malnutrition/index.cfm.

19. Durtschi, "Determining Deficiency Diseases Caused by Malnutrition."

20. Durtschi, "Determining Deficiency Diseases Caused by Malnutrition."

Chapter 3: Testing for and Treating Malnutrition

21. Hajjar et al., "Malnutrition in Aging."

22. Hajjar et al., "Malnutrition in Aging."

23. Hajjar et al., "Malnutrition in Aging."

Chapter 4: When Essential Nutrients Are Lacking

24. PBS, "Deadly Diseases: Malnutrition." www.pbs.org/wgbh/rxforsurvival/series/diseases/malnutrition.html.
25. John Heinerman, *Nature's Vitamins and Minerals*. Paramus, NJ: Prentice-Hall, 1998, p. 105.
26. Heinerman, *Nature's Vitamins and Minerals*, p. 275.
27. Bread for the World, "Obesity and Hunger." www.bread.org/learn/us-hunger-issues/obesity-and-hunger.html.

Chapter 5: Intentional Malnutrition: Eating Disorders

28. Eating Disorder Referral and Information Center, "Anorexia Nervosa." www.edreferral.com/anorexia_nervosa.htm.
29. Ann, interview with the author, 1990.
30. Eating Disorder Referral and Information Center, "Consequences of Eating Disorders." www.edreferral.com/consequences_of_ed.htm.
31. Grainne Smith, *Anorexia and Bulimia in the Family: One Parent's Practical Guide to Recovery*. West Sussex,UK: John Wiley and Sons, 2004, p. 34.
32. Smith, *Anorexia and Bulimia in the Family*, p. 13.
33. National Eating Disorders Association, "Causes of Eating Disorders." www.edap.org/p.asp?WebPage_ID=286&Profile_ID=41144.
34. Smith, *Anorexia and Bulimia in the Family*, p. 153.

Chapter 6: World Hunger: Crisis and Solutions

35. Loretta Schwartz-Nobel, *Growing Up Empty: The Hunger Epidemic in America*. New York: HarperCollins, 2002, pp. 4–5.
36. Bread for the World, "Hunger Facts: International." www.bread.org/learn/hunger-basics/hunger-facts-international.html.
37. Bread for the World, "Hunger Facts: International."

38. Quoted in UN News Center, "UN Food Agency Calls for Renewed Effort to Fight Hunger." www.un.org/apps/news/story.asp?NewsID=19749&Cr=Hunger&Cr1.

39. Quoted in Karen DeYoung, "Gates, Rockefeller Charities Join to Fight African Hunger," *Washington Post*, September 13, 2006, p. A1.

40. Bill and Melinda Gates Foundation, "New Hope for African Farmers." www.gatesfoundation.org/Global Development/Agriculture/RelatedInfo/AfricanFarmers.htm.

Glossary

albumin: Manufactured in the liver, a protein that keeps the blood from leaking out of the body's blood vessels and also contributes to tissue growth and healing. Bodily levels of albumin can be measured in a blood test called a serum albumin test.

anemia: A deficiency of red blood cells.

anorexia (anorexia nervosa): An eating disorder in which a person regularly self-starves and over time becomes abnormally thin.

beriberi: A deficiency disease caused by an inadequate intake of thiamine.

body mass index (BMI): A numerical expression of the relationship between weight and height, obtained by dividing a person's weight (in kilograms) by his or her height (in meters).

bulimia (bulimia nervosa): An eating disorder in which a person regularly eats unusually large amounts of food at one sitting and then vomits it up.

deficiency disease: A medical condition caused by inadequate consumption of micronutrients or macronutrients.

distorted body image: A condition in which a person does not see his or her own body as it really is.

follicular hyperkeratosis: A condition in which one's hair follicles stiffen for extended periods of time.

ketones: Substances that form when the body burns its own stores of fat to produce energy and that can sometimes be indicators of malnutrition.

kwashiorkor: A kind of malnutrition caused by a lack of protein.

macronutrients: Nutritional substances the body uses in large amounts, including protein, carbohydrates, and fats.

malnutrition: Lack of proper nutrients, brought about by eating too little food or too few specific nutrients.

marasmus: A kind of malnutrition in which someone consumes too little food overall and as a result lacks both protein and essential vitamins and minerals.

medical history: A series of questions and answers a doctor asks a patient in an effort to diagnose and treat a medical condition.

megestrol acetate: A steroid used in treating some forms of malnutrition.

metabolism: The series of processes by which the body converts food into energy.

micronutrients: Nutritional substances the body uses in very small amounts, including vitamins and minerals.

nandrolone: A steroid used to increase appetite.

obese: Grossly overweight.

pellagra: A deficiency disease caused by inadequate intake of niacin.

polysubstance use or abuse: Taking two or more drugs or medicines.

primary malnutrition: A condition in which an otherwise healthy person does not consume a sufficient amount of food or specific nutrients to maintain good health.

purge: To get rid of something. People with bulimia purge by vomiting up the food they have eaten.

rickets: A deficiency disease caused by an inadequate intake of vitamin D.

scurvy: A deficiency disease caused by an inadequate intake of vitamin C.

secondary malnutrition: A form of malnutrition that is a side effect of illness due to disease or injury.

steatorrhoeic hepatosis (or fatty liver): An excess buildup of fats in the liver.

toxic: Poisonous.

vitamins and minerals: Chemical substances used by the body in small amounts to maintain regular health.

xerosis: Dry skin.

Organizations to Contact

American Dietetic Association (ADA)
120 S. Riverside Plaza, Suite 2000
Chicago, IL 60606-6995
(800) 877-1600
Web site: www.eatright.org

The ADA provides the public and medical professionals with information about food, nutrition, and proper diet.

Food and Nutrition Information Center (FNIC)
National Agricultural Library
10301 Baltimore Ave., Rm. 105
Beltsville, MD 20705
(301) 504-5414
fax: (301) 504-6409

The FNIC provides information on proper nutrition, issues of weight and obesity, and eating disorders.

National Eating Disorders Association (NEDA)
603 Stewart St., Suite 803
Seattle, WA 98101
(800) 931-2237
e-mail: info@nationaleatingdisorders.org

The NEDA works to prevent and provide treatment for anorexia, bulimia, and binge eating.

National Institute on Alcohol Abuse and Alcoholism (NIAAA)
5635 Fishers Ln., MSC 9304
Bethesda, MD 20892-9304
Alcohol Abuse Hotline: (301) 443-3860
e-mail: niaaaweb-r@exchange.nih.gov

The NIAAA provides information about the consequences of alcohol abuse, including how it can lead to malnutrition.

National Institutes of Health (NIH)
9000 Rockville Pike
Bethesda, MD 20892
(301) 496-4000
e-mail: nihinfo@od.nih.gov

The NIH provide information about a wide range of medical diseases, conditions, and issues, including nutrition and conditions caused by lack of proper nutrition.

United Nations Children's Fund (UNICEF)
U.S. Fund for UNICEF
333 E. Thirty-eighth St.
New York, NY 10016
(212) 686-5522
fax: (212) 779-1679
e-mail: information@unicefusa.org

UNICEF promotes the health and human rights of children around the world, including providing programs that fight world hunger.

For Further Reading

Books

Editors of McGraw-Hill, *Nutrition and Wellness*. New York: McGraw-Hill, 2003. A comprehensive, useful synopsis of what constitutes proper nutrition and what does not.

Scott Ingram, *Want Fries with That? Obesity and the Supersizing of America*. New York: Franklin Watts, 2005. An excellent examination of the rise of obesity, which is closely related to the incidence of malnutrition in the United States.

Nancy J. Kolodny, *The Beginner's Guide to Eating Disorders*. Carlsbad, CA: Gurze, 2004. This well-written and easy-to-read overview is a good place to begin a study of eating disorders, which cause millions of people to become malnourished each year.

Howard D. Leathers and Phillips Foster, *The World Food Problem: Tackling the Causes of Undernutrition in the Third World*. Boulder, CO: Lynne Rienner, 2004. An enlightening look at the ongoing problem of world hunger.

Carol E. Normandi and Laurelee Roark, *Over It: A Teen's Guide to Getting Beyond Obsession with Food and Weight*. Novato, CA: New World Library, 2001. Provides some good advice to young people on how to avoid, cope with, and/or get help for eating disorders.

Loretta Schwartz-Nobel, *Growing Up Empty: The Hunger Epidemic in America*. New York: HarperCollins, 2002. Effectively chronicles the reality that malnutrition exists among millions of people in the United States, despite the country's great wealth.

Web Sites

KidsHealth (www.kidshealth.org). The article "Hunger and Malnutrition," which is part of the parents' section of this site, offers a general overview of the subject. In the teen section, the article "Vitamins and Minerals" is a useful synopsis of the major vitamins and minerals and their importance to nutrition.

National Institute of Mental Health (www.nimh.nih.gov/ Publicat/eatingdisorders.cfm). The article "Eating Disorders" provides an excellent introduction to the various eating disorders.

United Nations Children's Fund (www.unicef.org/nutrition /index_bigpicture.html). The article entitled "Nutrition: The Big Picture" provides an informative overview of the world hunger problem.

Index

Picture Credits

Cover photo: © iStockphoto.com/Jorge Delgado
Anatomical Travelogue/Photo Researchers, Inc., 34
AP Images, 9, 28, 32, 71, 77
© Beawiharta/Reuters/Corbis, 80
© Lester V. Bergman/Corbis, 56, 57
© Bettmann/Corbis, 54
Biophoto Associates/Photo Researchers, Inc., 52
Scott Camazine/Photo Researchers, Inc., 41
© Clouds Hills Imaging, Ltd. /Corbis, 30
CNRI/Photo Researchers, Inc., 21
© Corbis, 16
© Dennis Galante/Corbis, 69
Arthur Glauberman/Photo Researchers, Inc., 22
JI Unlimited, 60 (photo), 84 (photo)
Dr. P. Marazzi/Photo Researchers, Inc., 33
Will and Deni McIntyre/Photo Researchers, Inc., 47
© Jacques Pavlovsky/Sygma/Corbis, 15
Phanie/Photo Researchers, Inc., 44
© Chris Rainier/Corbis, 10
© Dr. Milton Reisch/Corbis, 53
© Jeffrey L. Rotman/Corbis, 58
© Warren Todaepa/Corbis, 86
© Catherine Ursillo/Photo Researchers, Inc. Reproduced
   by permission, 45
© Heiko Wolfraumdpa/Corbis, 67
Steve Zmina, 14, 60 (chart), 84 (chart)

About the Author

In addition to his numerous acclaimed volumes on ancient civilizations, historian Don Nardo has published several studies of modern scientific and medical discoveries and phenomena. Among these are *Germs*, *Atoms*, *Biological Warfare*, *Eating Disorders*, *Breast Cancer*, *Vaccines*, and biographies of scientists Charles Darwin and Tycho Brahe. Mr. Nardo lives with his wife, Christine, in Massachusetts.